The Canadian Poet Who Wrote Himself Whole

The Canadian Poet Who Wrote Himself Whole
Revealing the Poetics of Don Gutteridge

MSc Miguel Ángel Olivé Iglesias

First Edition

QuodSermo Publishing
www.HiddenBrookPress.com
QuodSermo@gmail.com

Title – The Canadian Poet Who Wrote Himself Whole
Subtitle – Revealing the Poetics of Don Gutteridge
Author – MSc Miguel Ángel Olivé Iglesias

Cover Design – Richard M. Grove
Cover Image – Richard M. Grove
Layout and Design – Richard M. Grove

Typeset in Garamond
Printed and bound in Canada

Library and Archives Canada Cataloguing in Publication

Title: The Canadian poet who wrote himself whole : revealing the poetics of Don Gutteridge / MSc Miguel Ángel Olivé Iglesias.
Names: Olivé Iglesias, Miguel Ángel, 1965- author.
Identifiers: Canadiana 20220166420 |
ISBN 9781989786574 (softcover)
Subjects: LCSH: Gutteridge, Don, 1937-—Criticism and interpretation.
Classification: LCC PS8513.U85 Z65 2022 |
DDC C813/.54—dc23

Acknowledgements

I thank God and The Virgin Mother for all the blessings in my life. I have prayed for me, my family, my friends, and I have been listened to. I have prayed for peace of mind, goodness, health, fortitude. He has always smiled on me, she has been always kind. That is why I live in trust, certainty and gratefulness. I cannot ask for more. Theirs is the best pulse of life, the best source for words.

I especially thank Don Gutteridge. When he was told I would write this book he gave full approval. It honors me. I also take my hat off for Richard Grove/Tai, the generous soul, the supportive friend no matter what. He has put his efforts, budget, trust and love into so many me-related projects. I will never have enough words – English, Spanish or any other language – to express my profound gratitude to him. A word of endless appreciation to Adislenis, the eBook designer, who never says no to her friends.

I thank Amanda, my daughter, who lights up my life in so many ways. I still marvel how I could even breathe before she was born.

I deeply thank my wife for her encouragement and hours of self-imposed silence so I could, once more and always, put my mind at ease, focus and write this book and so many others.

Table of Contents

Dedicated to

Anne, Tom and Don

Richard Marvin Grove/Tai, for his passion, support, love and commitment to culture, Canadian literature. For believing in me

All poets, for their contribution to love and life

My family, for everything

My students, for being a significant part of my life

My friends and colleagues, for their encouragement and trust

The Author/Editor
MSc Miguel Ángel Olivé Iglesias

Dance

... a blank page I wrote
myself upon with words. Don Gutteridge
Words dancing. Ariadne Sawyer
This poem is a dance, a ritual. John B. Lee

Words. They lie dormant
waiting until the time is ripe

then they wake
sway gently at first
grow wings, fly
onto blank spaces of paper

torrential in the heart
urging the pencil
nourished by life.

They follow ancient rhythms,
a ritual into the most fruitful of moments
a dance
of poet
and words.

Miguel Ángel Olivé Iglesias

Literary critics will have much to say about Gutteridge's uniquely Canadian vision. I am content that his poetry is accessible, unobtrusive, delights the ear, stirs the heart and even enters into the soul. It is the art that mirrors inner life

R. G. Moyles, The University of Alberta
In The Journal of Canadian Poetry

Nothing short of a stroke could stop me from writing poetry… I seem to dream poems and wake up writing them... I am very fortunate that the Muse has never let me down.

Don Gutteridge

Introduction

The Canadian Poet Who Wrote Himself Whole put my intellectual capacity and my literary acumen to the test. The reason was a good one, my friend Richard Marvin Grove/Tai asked me to approach Don´s vast literary output in a more comprehensive volume of his life and work.

Another much valid reason was that writing more extensively about an icon like Gutteridge posed a delicate challenge to me, a modest Cuban professor treading on the paths of Canadian literature. Accepting the invitation involved rereading the books I had already approached, embarking on a new journey with many more books Don and Richard generously sent me, and retracing my paper on Don in my book *Five Canadian Poets: Analytical Essays on James Deahl, John B. Lee, Don Gutteridge, Glen Sorestad, A. F. Moritz* (QuodSermo Publishing, 2021), in a critical, fresh revision to enrich its contents and re-channel its purport.

Readers must be aware that what I have said in these pages is my personal interpretation (and feelings he stirred) of Don´s work. On the other hand, my unpretentious insights are accurately propped, developed and coloured by expert quotations and references I include, by Don´s interesting comments about his life, his technique, influences and inspirations gathered from an extensive interview I did with him by email and by a largely illustrative collection of his full poems (or excerpts) from his many books, thanks mostly to the bigheartedness of Hidden Brook Press and Don, and last but not least by Kimberley Grove´s input and fine accounts of Gutteridge´s life and work.

I foresaw a huge undertaking ahead of me but in the end I took it: Gutteridge and Canadian literature deserved it. The fact that a publisher, writer and literary promoter like Grove trusted me on this task, gave me the self-esteem and impulse I needed to set sails again into Don´s oceanic oeuvre. I was also honored by Don´s approval. His agreement was my definitive motivation. I am so glad I said yes. I am so proud of what Richard Grove, Kimberley Grove, I and most of all Don, without whose works and assistance we would have been at a loss, have put together in this book. The journey turned out to be one of pleasure, rediscovery, relearning and ethical-aesthetic enlightenment.

May readers feel likewise reading this book and absorbing the unobjectionably literary, educational, tasteful, evocative, kindhearted and elegant worth it possesses – not because I wrote it or we made it come to fruition but because it collects in a single volume (which by no means exhausts an examination of Gutteridge´s work and contribution to literature) the treasure that is Don Gutteridge´s literary heritage.

Biographical Notes on Don Gutteridge

by Kimberley Grove

Don Gutteridge started his writing career when he was confined to his bed for nine months with rheumatic fever when he should have been enjoying Grade 2. Don was never lazy so he read enough books to fill his imagination and learn the craft of writing. When he returned to school in Grade 3 he wrote a story for his teacher Miss McDonald. She praised it so much that he realized he was on to something. And he has been writing ever since.

He has published 45 poetry books, 13 novels, 12 mysteries and 11 non-fiction books, as well as numerous articles. In his own words he talks about the thrill of his first published poem in a respected literary magazine, *The Fiddlehead*. "In the Fall of 1960, my wife Anne and I, both starting to teach that month in the Elmira High School, and decided to live in the nearby village of Elora. We moved into the servants' quarters of the old George Drew homestead and began our married life. I now made a life-changing decision. Having had poems published in Western's literary magazine, I decided I would start sending the few new short lyrics I was writing to *The Fiddlehead* poetry magazine, edited by Professor Fred Cogswell. Tucking several poems into my case, I walked to the local post office (there was no mail delivery in the village) and, both thrilled and fearful, I mailed the poems to be judged, not by student editors, but by some literary man or woman of taste, 2000 miles away. Every morning for two months, I walked into the village square to check my mail. I watched the leaves go gold and crimson and finally fall and drift. There was no response to my maiden gambit. I felt crestfallen and began to regret announcing to Anne that I was planning to become a published poet. Sometime in the chill of November, there was a letter for me, my own self-addressed envelope. I let it sit on the kitchen table awhile and, when Anne was abroad, found the courage to open it. One of my poems had been accepted, a six-line fragment I had been debating sending, but with it a short note in Professor Cogswell's scrawl, to say the poem would be published in the Spring edition of the magazine. I was a published poet on my first try. And thus began a fifty-year relationship with Fred Cogswell, a luminary of our literary world. Within three years, he would publish three of the mid-length narrative poems I had begun to write and, in 1968, my first published book, *Riel*. I was no longer an apprentice. That Autumn of 1960 was one of the seminal experiences of my life." The *Riel* book was such a masterpiece that CBC picked up on the genius of the writing and did a radio drama of it.

There were quite a few stories in Don's own history that prove the saying, "Life is stranger than fiction." His maternal grandmother, Lilly Smith, met his grandfather in Detroit. She had been married once before. "When she was sixteen, her father wagered her in a craps game, lost and handed his daughter over to a William Campbell, whom she was forced to marry." Campbell abandoned her when Roy Campbell was born, so she divorced him.

"My maternal grandfather (John McWatters, a.resident of Sarnia, Ontario) worked as a carpenter until he retired in the Spring of 1939. He worked at odd jobs, and one day after finishing a job and being paid, he headed straight to his regular bootleggers, where he partied with friends well into the night. Sometime towards morning he stepped onto the porch of the house for a smoke and was struck viciously from behind. Unconscious, he collapsed face-down in the garden. Too inebriated to move his head, he suffocated and died there. The inquest, written up in lurid detail in *The Sania Observer*, concluded that my grandfather was murdered by a person or persons unknown. The coroner said he had never heard such lying in a courtroom." In addition to Don's mother, Grace, Don's Uncle George was born into the McWatters' family.

"Uncle George was a brilliant man. At age twenty-five he was CEO of a Detroit bakery. Unfortunately, he had the McWatters gambling instinct. While working in Detroit he got tangled up with the local mob. Nothing happened until a few years later, when he had married and returned to Sarnia, and raised two sons. He began working for the Sarnia City Bus Company as a bus driver. He was given the Point Edward route and while waiting at the terminal two blocks from my home, he would ask me to get on, feed me peanuts, drive around the block and let me off. Within a short time, he became president of the company. At the same time, he got into the debt of the Detroit mob, who threatened to break his legs if he did not pay up. Desperate, he embezzled the money from the company, paid the mob, but was caught when the books were examined. They thought so highly of him, that he was not charged, merely let go. He vowed never to gamble again, but as gambling was all he had left, he set up a gambling den (illegal at that time) above the Cozy Café in Sarnia, dealt the cards (to the higher ups in the Refinery and Polymer plant and other respectable bigwigs) and took five per cent of the pot. His wife, my Aunt Grace, made and served the sandwiches. I heard about Aunt Grace but never saw her in those days because, ill with some mysterious ailment (depression likely), she took to her bed for two years and never left it. I finally met her in the 1960s when she and Uncle George came to London to visit my mother."

Uncle George who married a Grace, the same name as his sister, had a son Dick when they were living in Detroit, but they moved to Canada shortly after but never mentioned to their son that he was born in the United States. One night in 1951 when Dick was in Port Huron, Michigan, enjoying the night life, he was stopped at the border by Customs and told that his draft number had come up and he was sent immediately to Korea. "Dick served in Korea for a year and a half in the thick of the fighting. When he returned he was a changed man. He never married."

Some of these stories made it into Don's writing with some poetic license. In addition, he used his father figure for the main character of his first novel, Bus-Ride. His father (William Ernest Charles Gutteridge) was an excellent hockey player, well- known in Southern Ontario, and scouted by the Detroit Red Wings. However, in those early days of hockey, the players weren't paid like they are today and instead of playing hockey for a living, he signed up with the Royal Canadian Air Force (RCAF). During some of his years of service, the family lived in an apartment above the grandparents in Point Edward (a village near Sarnia) just across the border from the United States. If a person can fall in love with a place, then Don did just that. Much of his writing was based in Point Edward and the people he knew there. His father had moved the family away from the village to Sarnia's Township when he finished his time in the RCAF. "The move into the lonely countryside, away from my home village, was devastating for me. For two years my brother and I, every second week, walked to the train station and caught the bus to Point Edward, where we stayed with Gran and Gramps, and tried to keep up the fraying friendships that had been so much a part of my life." The other hardship of his life was his disconnect with his father. "We had a difficult time bonding: he was a superb athlete, I wasn't." His father was away so much that eventually he left the family and moved to Calgary where he got work as a taxidermist. His parents divorced and his father also started to drink heavily which eventually killed him. The main character of Don's first apprentice novel was based on his father. He sent his book to Jack McClelland who liked it, but was concerned that the entire book had not one word of dialogue. He went on to learn that aspect of his craft when Alice Munro explained that dialogue comes naturally from the creation of strong characters put in the same room.

Don's Dad then moved the family to Chatham, Ontario. After studying at Chatham Collegiate Institute, he was accepted in 1956 to the University of Western Ontario where he received an Honours Degree in English Language and Literature. Following that, he had the opportunity to teach English to students at the Grades 11, 12 and 13 level at Elmira District High School. In addition to realizing that he had found a profession that he loved, he also met the woman of his dreams, Margaret Anne Barnett, the Home Economics teacher. "I proposed on a snowy night in February 1961 in Anne's new Volkswagon. We were married by a judge in Guelph and attended a small reception for us by school friends and my mother and brother. We rented the back half (servant's quarters) of a big house (the old Drew homestead) and began our married life, driving each day from Elora to Elmira District High School. Many weekends we drove to Toronto for musicals and plays at the O'Keefe Centre. It was a wonderful winter and spring. Over 85% of my Grade 13 students passed their provincial English exam."

In 1963 his work on a M.A. was halted because he realized that he needed to obtain employment to support his newborn son, William John Barnett Gutteridge. His daughter, Catherine Anne Gutteridge, was born in 1966. Family life was a blessing as it gave him the opportunity to see a lot of Canada as they enjoyed family outings and camping.

He returned to his passion of teaching at Beck Collegiate in London. This work led to his teaching English Methods to prospective High School teachers for 25 years at

Althouse, which became a Faculty of Education at University of Western Ontario. It is easy to see that his love of teaching benefited his students, too, as he still is in contact with some of them today. He also wrote 10 academic books that will undoubtedly help others that share his love of teaching.

Bored with retirement, he wrote a twelve-volume mystery series, *The Marc Edwards Mysteries*, with four publishers over a twelve-year period (2003-2015). This engaged him with his other favourite subject, History, as these books creatively cover the story of an ensign, Marc Edwards, from 1836-1841. They describe Canada in a way that is easy to digest for anyone interested in that period of our country's history, as he did a great deal of research to get the facts correct about the times, although his main character is fictional.

When Don talks about the special moments in his life, he refers to his children's births and the wonderful marriage he shared with Anne. His joy extends from his grandparents to his six grandchildren. This book is dedicated to Tom, the grandchild that lived with him and Anne for six years and dedicated a large amount of time to reading and talking about his grandfather's works. Tom created several podcasts (https://thereandthen.podbean.com/) in which the public can learn more about Don's thought process when writing. You can hear the enjoyment Don had in doing the interviews. At some points, you hear his laughter when talking about his characters, as though he gets as much enjoyment from them as his reader will.

"It's been a full life." And the list of his works that follows is proof of that:

Poetry:

– *Riel: A Poem For Voices*, Fiddlehead Poetry Books: Fredericton, 1968; and Van Nostrand Reinhold: Toronto, 1972
– *The Village Within*, Fiddlehead: Fredericton, 1970
– *Death At Quebec and Other Poems*, Fiddlehead: Fredericton, 1971
– Perspectives: Poems Toward a Biography, Pennywise Press, London, Ontario, 1971
– *Saying Grace: An Elegy*, Fiddlehead: Fredericton, 1972
– *Coppermine: The Quest For North*, Oberon: Ottawa, 1973
– *Borderlands*, Oberon: Ottawa, 1975
– *Tecumseh*, Oberon: Ottawa, 1976
– *A True History of Lambton County*, Oberon: Ottawa, 1977
– *God's Geography*, Brick Books: London, 1982
– *The Exiled Heart; Selected Narratives*, Oberon: Ottawa, 1986
– *Love in the Wintertime*, Oberon: Ottawa, 1990
– *Flute Music in the Cello's Belly*, Moonstone: Goderich, 1997
– *Bloodlines*, Oberon: Ottawa, 2001
– *Something More Miraculous*, Oberon: Ottawa, 2004

– *Still Magical*, Oberon: Ottawa, 2007
– *Coming Home*, Oberon: Ottawa, 2011
– *The Way It Was*, Friesen Press: Vancouver, 2014
– *Tidings*, Black Moss Press: Windsor, 2015
– *Peripheries*, (ebook) First Choice Books: Victoria, 2016
– *Inundations*, Hidden Brook Press: Brighton, 2016
– *The Blue Flow Below*, Black Moss Press: Windsor, 2017
– *The Sands of Canatara,* (ebook) First Choice Books: Victoria, 2017
– *Inklings,* Black Moss Press: Windsor, 2017
– *The Village Within* ,(re-issue, ebook) First Choice Books: Victoria, 2017
– *Cameron Lake,* (ebook) First Choice Books: Victoria, 2018
– *Home Ground*, Hidden Brook Press: Brighton, 2018
– *Two Dozen for Anne*, First Choice books, Victoria, 2018
– *Bereft: Poems for my Beloved*, First Choice Books, Victoria, 2018
– *Another Poem For Anne*," First Choice Books, Victoria, 2018
– "*Days Worth the Telling*, Black Moss Press, Windsor, 2018
– "*The Breath of My Being*, First Choice Books, Victoria, 2018
– "*Foster's Pond*," Borealis, Ottawa, 2019
– "*The Star-Brushed Horizon*, Hidden Brook Press: Brighton, 2019
– *Mara's Lamp*, Black Moss Press: Windsor, 2019
– *Impious Whims: Selected Poems*, Borealis Press, 2019
– "*In the Rarefied Regions of the Heart*, Hidden Brook Press: Brighton, 2020
– "*Point Taken: Collected Poems 2014-2020*, Hidden Brook Press: Brighton, 2020
– *By and By*, With John B. Lee. Hidden Brook Press: Brighton, 2020
– *The Derelict Heart*, Hidden Brook Press: Brighton, 2020
– *Invincible Ink*, Hidden Brook Press: Brighton, 2020
– *Into the Milkweed Meadow*, Hidden Brook Press: Brighton, 2021
– *Where Rivers Run Deep*, Hidden Brook Press: Brighton, 2001
– *More Boding Than Blood*, Hidden Brook Press: Brighton, 2021
– *The Ardent Dark*, Hidden Brook Press: Brighton, 2021

Fiction:

– *Bus-Ride*, Nairn publishing: Nairn, 1974
– *All in Good Time*, Black Moss Press: Windsor, 1980
– *St. Vitus Dance*, Drumlin: London, 1986
– *Shaman's Ground*, Drumlin: London, 1988
– *How the World Began*, Moonstone: Goderich, 1991

– *Summer's Idyll*, Oberon: Ottawa, 1993
– *Winter's Descent*, Oberon: Ottawa, 1996
– *Bewilderment*, Borealis: Ottawa, 2000
– *The Perilous Journey of Gavin the Great*, Borealis Press: Ottawa, 2010
– *The Rebellion Mysteries*, Simon and Schuster: Toronto, 2012
– *Lily's Story*,(e-book). Bev Editions: Toronto, 2013 (Print edition 2014)
– *Constable Garrett and the Dead Ringer*, Tellwell: Victoria, 2016
– *Lily Fairchild*, Tablo publications, 2019

Marc Edwards Mysteries:
– *Turncoat*, McClelland and Stewart: Toronto, 2003
– *Solemn Vows*, McClelland and Stewart: Toronto, 2003
– *Vital Secrets*, Trinity: Saint John, 2007
– *Dubious Allegiance*, Simon and Schuster: Toronto, 2012
– *Bloody Relations*, Simon and Schuster: Toronto, 2013
– *Death of a Patriot*, Simon and Schuster: Toronto, 2014
– *The Bishop's Pawn*, Tablo Publishing: Melbourne, 2021
– *Desperate Acts*, Tablo Publishing: Melbourne, 2021
– *Unholy Alliance*, Tablo Publishing: Melbourne, 2021
– *Mnor Corruption*, Tablo Publishing: Melbourne*, 2021*
– *Governing Passion,* Tablo Publishing: Melbourne, 2021
– *The Widow's Demise,* Tablo Publishing: Melbourne, 2021

The six mysteries above were also published as ebooks by Bev Editions in 2015

Non-Fiction:
– *Rhetoric: A Unified Approach to Literary Curricula*, OISE: Toronto, 1970 (contributor)
– *Language and Expression*, McClelland and Stewart: Toronto, 1970
– *The Country of the Young*, The Althouse Press: London, 1978
– *Mountain and Plain*, Anthology. McClelland and Stewart: Toronto, 1978
– *Rites of Passage*, Anthology. McClelland and Stewart: Toronto, 1979
– *Brave Season*, The Althouse Press: London, 1983
– *Incredible Journeys*, The Althouse Press: London, 1986 and 1990
– *The Dimension of Delight*, The Althouse Press: London, 1988
– *Stubborn Pilgrimage*, Our Schools/Our Selves: Toronto, 1994
– *Teaching English*, Lorimer: Toronto, 2000
– *The Myth Alive: Essays in Canadian Literature and Poetics*, First Choice Books: Victoria, 2015

Bard

I find it hard to imagine
a life without the wizardry
of words: the nuances of nouns
and verbs surging: pinned
in the prism of a poem, where rhyme
has its reasons and rhythm is what
the heart hears in the silence
between beats and simile
has its seasons, and I was born
to pain and poetry, and longed
to embrace the arcane business
of being a bard.

Don Gutteridge

Development

Flashbacks

As early as 1943 – six years after the iconic Canadian writer I am reviewing in this book, Don Gutteridge, was born – E. K. Brown referred in *On Canadian Poetry* to Canadian literature in the following terms: "Canadian literature I shall understand writing by those who having been born in Canada passed a considerable number of their best creative years in this country, and also writing by those who, wherever they may have been born, once arrived in Canada did important creative work and led much of their literary life among us." Gutteridge, belongs to the first, having-been-born-in-Canada group. And Gutteridge has certainly had a long string of "creative years."

Later, Brown stated that "The serious Canadian writer has a choice among three modes of combining the pursuit of literature with success in keeping alive and fed. He may emigrate… He may earn his living by some non-literary pursuit… He may while continuing to reside in Canada become, economically at least, a member of another nation and civilization…" *(ibidem)* Gutteridge is within the category of "serious Canadian writer" and, while pursuing both paths almost at the same time, he earned his living – until retirement, when he devoted fully to writing, especially to poetry – by some non-literary, yet related, pursuit.

Brown goes further in saying that: "… a single man of genius might emerge and express himself… A great literature is the flowering of a great society, a mature and adequate society." *(ibidem)* Therefrom we can safely ascertain that the fruit-bearing combination of writer and society, that is, individuals and society, within a favorable context, can thrive as they drink from the inexhaustible sources provided by their pioneer writers, context, talent and experiences. Gutteridge has done that.

Gutteridge´s answer to my question about his own themes and how they imbricate with the national Canadian spirit of poetry was the following: "I write on many themes over a long life, but more recently I have concentrated on memories of childhood experiences, friends, romantic crushes and sexual awakening, on elegies for my beloved wife and grandson who've passed away recently, tributes to friends and poems, about the process of writing poems."

For many reasons, Gutteridge fits comfortably in Canadian poet Antony Di Nardo´s maxim, "Write what you know. Write what you love, what you care about…" Gutteridge´s choice of themes has led him through an extraordinary career as an acclaimed writer. He has extensively written about what he knows and holds dear.

His attitude towards life and poetry is evidenced in his poem "Defy," "... poetry is both bliss and consolation, a way of speaking to the world that subsumes both shy and defy." Don, like many other poets, beholds poetry as communication. Every poet understands that poems do speak to people, they state something, they grant happiness in the realization of the self, and bring comfort to the poet's soul, to his/her need of expression and relief.

Gutteridge had his origins early in childhood. In an email he commented to me: "I wrote my first story at age 8 and my first poem at age 12, and I've been writing almost daily ever since. When a poem "comes right" I am happy with it. I give it a day and a second look and that's it."

This is what he tells us in his bio: "In October 1944 I contracted rheumatic fever and was hospitalized for a week. The high fever opened the valves of my heart... Dr. Christie... ordered complete bed rest for seven months. I was a precocious reader and spent my bedridden hours reading whatever I could find. I never left the bed once until May of 1945."

The year 1945 marks then the auspicious beginnings of this outstanding Canadian author. School contexts and his teachers also influenced him: "I returned to school to finish grade two with the support of my wonderful teacher, Mrs. Young, who brought me homework to keep me up to date. I wrote my first story for Miss McDonald, my grade three teacher, (and a poem about it in God's Geography). From that time on I found a group of fast friends in the village whom I have put into poems and novels. It was a great life (as the books show)." Eventually, during the 1960s, he became a teacher; teaching became a passion for him: "I instantly fell in love with teaching."

Gutteridge has intensely and extensively recreated his "great life" in his books. His poetry and novels have brought to us years of his life. We wonder, as we read about him, if there was any event or character he has left out.

When we read his work, we cannot fail in finding all his experiences outlined, elaborated on, colored in the excellent penmanship we enjoy across his oeuvre. Names of people, places (Point Edward being an unavoidable one), schools, locations, flash through the hundreds of pages we could bind together in all his books.

As I mentioned above, Gutteridge had an almost unisonous start at writing poetry and prose. In his bio he recalls this gift always stayed with him: "I thought that if I were to become a novelist, I had better learn to write dialogue. (I learned later in the decade by taking the advice of Alice Munro: that dialogue comes naturally from the creation of strong characters put in the same room.) Meanwhile I had had my first poem published in a real magazine: "This Maple in my Fallen Yard" in the Fiddlehead (1961 or 1962 and republished in *The Village Within*). Encouraged I started to write both short lyrics about

Point Edward and several long poems about the Jesuits in Huronia, Champlain and LaSalle."

By this time, Gutteridge was collecting what he had planted. Novels, poems, and substantial advice given by Munro started to chart his course. The pieces of advice and influences he had were obvious and durable: "Favourite authors are Hopkins, Dickinson, Hardy, Alice Munro and many others. I am from a working-class family and there were few books in the house. I was encouraged to write by my aunt."

A key "icebreaker" in the literary world was *God's Geography*, about which Michael O Nowlan said, "Don Gutteridge, who has established himself as an authentic voice for Canadian literature, has produced an unusual text in *God's Geography*. It may be classified as a book of poetry, which it is; but it goes far beyond that dimension. It is really an album of memories… *God's Geography* is a stirring piece of work that provokes memory. It is the kind of word-experience one would obtain by translating the family album into verse. There is much here for many readings. Like his memories, Gutteridge's work strengthens with time."

He started to write short lyrics about Point Edward and long poems about the Jesuits in Huronia, Champlain and LaSalle. In 1967 he read *Strange Empire* by John Kinsey Howard and began work on a series of poems about Louis Riel. This is how he remembers it: "… eventually (I finished it) as *Riel: A Poem for Voices*. I sent it off to Fred Cogswell at Fiddlehead and he agreed to publish 500 copies if I would subsidize the printing. Somehow, with a growing family and a new apartment in Inglewood Park, I squeezed out $200 and my first of more than 65 books was published in 1968. I was an author."

Making poetry out of history

Riel: A Poem for Voices, a historical narrative poem published in 1972 by Van Nostrand Reinhold Ltd., came after an "accidental" occurrence while Don was watching TV: "… I remember being fascinated by the play, the story, and the man." The book was a result of both passion and meticulous study. Upon reading G. F. Stanley's biography of Riel and John Kinsey Howard's *Strange Empire: The Story of Louis Riel*, he furthered on the topic. As he stated in his Afterword, he was "making poetry out of history." *(ibidem)*

I wish to quote a small fragment from this formidable book just as a brief example of how spiritual and influential it is. The fragment speaks of the Métis connection with earth, the rooted conceptions they had, a bond that accompanied Riel all his life:

They were walking: as a Métis always walked
Because a man could feel the Mother Earth through the palms
Of his feet, and know the firmness of her flesh
And the great unturning heart at the centre of her…

Readers will relish in the spirituality of Don's words, the deep-seated recognition of the earth's significance, acknowledging it as an animate being.
Oberon Press published in 1973 his *Coppermine*. It is a narrative book whose center can be initially elucidated in the fragment below. There is transcendence, history and fine imagery in these few lines:

Matonabbee speaking
"Where the mouth of the grand river opens
To swallow the sea, lies the Copper-mine:
And they say the metal sits there in chunks
As big as a bison's flank…

Borderlands, Oberon Press (1975), is a story based on facts. John Jewitt was a prisoner of the Nootkas during three years until he was rescued. Gutteridge took that and turned it into the poem we have. On the book's back cover we read: "His (Jewitt's) remarkable story is the point of departure for the moving poem."

Borderlands is indeed a touching poem. Rich imagery stands out in it. How it ends, Maquina's (Chief of the Nootkas) words, stays with us linguistically – for its expressive means – and culturally – for its impact, vision, wisdom and resolved exhortation:

We are the people
of the coast, we
make an edge
against the sea
My body is a beginning,
a coast of skin
for the sea-dream
of my race
Let us inhabit
all borderlands
let us sing our morning-songs
before the sea rises
to claim her coast

Oberon Press continues publishing Gutteridge. In 1976 the public is offered *Tecumseh*. On the book's back cover we read: "Gutteridge is the kind of poet who can make poetry that is at once public and passionate, at once true to the actual human event and epic in scale, solemn, prophetic." Passionate, human, somber and visionary is the entire book, embodied in the closing piece:

This dawn-light is
ember-thin, it
quickens and

dismembers
me
I am fading
into the bleached
bone-beauty of
poems
I am everywhere
photographed in the
darkest rooms
I am the
passionate statue
in each of your parks
I am the
poet in his pure
air
(remember and
beware)

Gutteridge's writing career, academic and literary, moved on. He recalls in his bio the publications of his books: "… published… by Oberon, the most successful small literary publisher in Canada at that time. I felt I had arrived as a poet (and a minor novelist) and I continued to publish papers on educational theory and practice in English throughout my twenty-five-year career…"

During what he terms "a full life," Don has kept on writing and printing his work with different publishers: Oberon, Brick Books, Black Moss Press, Bev Editions, Moonstone, and Borealis. After retiring in 1993, he devoted himself to feverishly write: "I retired in October 1993. Bored with retirement, I started in on what became a twelve-volume mystery series, *The Marc Edwards Mysteries*, with four publishers over a twelve-year period (2003-2015).

These would be the last prose I would write. But I started writing poems again…" In 2017 First Choice Books reissued Don's *The Village Within*, an original 1970 Fiddlehead Books publication. The book is subtitled "poems towards a biography," which gives us an exact notion of the themes approached in it and the book's general tone. Some of the original poems were removed from this print, a decision made by Gutteridge because "not all of the poems now live up to my standard." He settled with the remaining poems, reproduced untouched.

Within the rich variety we find in the book, we have "This Maple in my Fallen Yard," a piece Don recalls as his "first poem published in a real magazine…" From it, here is an excerpt, the last stanza. Readers will absorb right away the solidity of a poem that stands the test of time and shows a rapidly maturing poet:

This maple in my fallen yard

dies a thousand lives
that old bones unmarrowed
on the cross of fallen leaves
can pull yet another spring
from the harrowed earth
of this my fallen world.

A brief, grave poem, made of various pieces, is "Some Thoughts for November." I chose the closing one, number 6, for its shortness yet also for its Emily Dickinson ring in mood and compactness. Gutteridge considers her a transcendental poet and quotes her at the beginning of the book:

When winter comes
there will be time, perhaps,
for lesser deaths.

Lily Fairchild

In 2014 *Lily's Story* was published by Don's agent under the imprimatur of Bev Editions. In 2019 he revised the novel and it was reissued as *Lily Fairchild.* Tablo Publishing, as Gutteridge said to me, "did the honours." An unquestionably outstanding and well-established poet, Don Gutteridge shows the rich tessiture of his writing in this superb, heart-touching piece of prose. The novel is an ode to sacrifice and endurance, to determination and courage, to freedom of thought and act, to faith magnificently worded in one of the book's final meditations: "… belief is a hard flame to extinguish…" In his words, "I wanted to write an historical novel (that abiding interest) from a woman's point of view…"

As a reader, I don't need a more suitable way to connect with a book than the one chosen by the author, as he starts by describing Lily's childhood settings, packed with family details:

> "*Lily was glad to be in the comfort of the trees' canopy. It was cozy here, like the cabin with Papa's fire blazing… While outside, heard only by her, the snow sang to the wind and no one in the world was lonely… She would surprise Papa at his work, celebrate another tree felled, and laugh when he swept her up and twirled her around, saying 'Lady Fair Child, may I have the pleasure of this dance?*"

The opening line in the book, "*Something stirred in the darkness ahead*," can be considered premonitory of what would befall Lily - prefaced in her Mama being sick. I value the allusions to Old Samuels' mumbled stories, a thoughtfully depicted character in both personality and language, an element that is appreciated in Gutteridge's choice of all dialogues, idioms, turns, graphic representation of speech, etc., which speaks highly of his meticulous studies to write the novel. Furthermore, at the threshold of Chapter 6

Gutteridge displays still another ominous act, "*I'm...Lily... Papa sent me... Sensing the bewilderment in the woman's face, Lil's heart sank. She fought against the faintness and vertigo as best she could, but it felt as if her bones had melted outright in a treacherous sun.*"

Exploiting these factors, Gutteridge prepares the reader for the avalanche of events unfurling from his pen. In many ways those early chores and experiences Lily, seven years old, had to assume and learn from molded her charisma, and may have given her strength to face the hardships and setbacks she would encounter along the way.
Two especially tender-sad moments come to us with the mother's "Let's have tea, little-one" incident when she tells Lily of her and Papa's previous life and how they came to a new country, and the scene with the cameo pendant with a silver chain that Lily's mother showed her:

> "*With a start, Lily recognized her own eyes. "Your grandmother." Mama's eyes filled with tears. She reached into the box again. "I saved this, out of the storm."*
> *She held up a gold chain on the end of which dangled a slender cross no more than half an inch long. Instinctively Lily leaned forward and the crucifix settled on her throat as if it had always expected to be there.*"

Auspiciously, this moving minute comes back to us at the end. *Lily Fairchild* finely chronicles, in its status as historical fiction, a period – rather a succession of periods – in the Canadian past that approaches natives' life – stylishly accompanied by the use of words coming from their languages, what brings the reader closer to the textual atmosphere – and sketches crisscrossing seeds that grew into the Canada we have today. Alongside, Gutteridge remains loyal, and constantly refers to one of the central motifs in Canadian writers, nature. He is faithful as well to his excellent treatment of family themes – skillfully addressed too in his poetry – placed either in the 1850s or in more contemporary contexts.

Another welcome virtue in the book is place references constantly being made – a tribute to Al Purdy's devotion to Canadian geography? – which play an important role throughout the novel, not just spatially but also from a historic-contextual perspective. More significantly, Gutteridge's accounts are the result of deep research to recreate locations and situations accurately.

Despite Lily's misfortunes and hard times, Gutteridge does stimulate the reader with some high peaks in her life in the form of her Aunt Bridie – family:
"*Bridie wanted to be severe but couldn't manage it...*" (Her Aunt enrolled Lily in Common School, giving Lily up as help around the house), and:

> "*Don't you fret about it, child," Bridie soothed. "Not much learnin' goes on in schools anyway. Come September, we'll teach you to read proper.*
> *She was looking at Lily now. "Remember this: We're not gonna spend all our life chewin' dirt.*"
> (Bridie gave Lily consolation after humiliation in school).

Once more, Gutteridge leans confidently on family ties to channel these two emotional instances in the novel. A most delicate matter becomes the centerpiece in the story when Lily gets pregnant. Such occurrence in the late 19th century would certainly be critical for a woman, given the epoch, which I won't advance here, of course. From this incident up to the dénouement, readers will be taken on a carrousel ride, going up, going down with Lily's predicaments. Were it not enough, Gutteridge gives us a soul-rending scene in Chapter 12:

> *"I do love you, Tom."*
> *"Then you'll marry me?"*
> *Lily looked away, then back. "I can't," she said.*
> *"But why?"*
> *She felt the full weight of his hurt and her own. "I can't marry a soldier."*

This is Lily. The book is masterfully filled with wise dialogue and monologue, with profound reflections, introspective and clear intentions to teach and leave an imprint on the reader. I have enjoyed Gutteridge's way of dealing with history in the making, blended with memories and an intensely personal story. These ingredients will please the most demanding of readers.

Home Ground

2018 was the year Hidden Brook Press published *Home Ground.* While I cannot go over each poem, I will focus on those that more strongly appealed to me and my own memories. This is what I call a close-significance approach. I comment on poems that stimulated evocations of my life and my own transit from childhood to adulthood. No significant experience and anecdote escaped Don, positive or negative, blissful or hurtful. Significant means to me that something leaves a mark; it teaches and encourages learning and channels what is learned towards an education and an attitude for life. Don Gutteridge opens his book with "Black Lake." There is light in the poem, quietness and peace: "unruffled, silvered surface," "ravishing red dot," "a pair of loons undulated," "sunny butterfly fluttering."

The poet praises the painter, Gerald Parker, and adds his personal poetic "strokes" by detailed descriptions for the reader. While the title includes "Black," there is overwhelming beauty beyond blackness achieved by painter and poet. We notice instances of alliteration in the poem: "lustrous light to lavish on Black Lake's...," "silvered surface, so," "loons ululated on the cusp of lust and the little stream..."

Alliteration builds a melodic effect into the utterance and creates an emotional atmosphere, very much in line with the poets' purpose. "Alliteration in the English language is deeply rooted in the traditions of English folklore... alliteration as a structural device... has shown remarkable continuity. It is frequently used... not only in verse..." *(Taken from Stylistics. I. R. Galperin. 1981)* Let's read the entire piece:

After a painting by Gerald Parker
One alabaster moon
was not enough lustrous
light to lavish on Black
Lake's unruffled,
silvered surface, so you
added a ravishing red
dot above the very
spot where a pair of loons
ululated on the cusp of lust
and the little stream feeding
filigree never slackened
its pace, and just to subvert
the scene you drew a sunny
butterfly fluttering
on monogrammed wings
over the outcrop
where we stopped to wonder
if this was all a dream.

"Moon Over Monk" shows instances of alliteration: "Mara's lamp… mellowing its light along…," "gently gendered," among others, plus other stylistic devices that embellish and give emotional connotation to the poem: a simile, ("the moon sits in the horizon") "like a serene replica of Mara's lamp." The moon is a leitmotif in Don's poetry and imagery, and accompanies his memories. This time, it reminds him of Mara – both lights will now show the way, together or alternately. The poet reminisces of his childhood games and "the sacred place where we play." Here, the full poem:

The moon over Monk Street
sits above the horizon
like a serene replica
of Mara's lamp, each
mellowing its light along
the sacred place where we play
our gently gendered games
in embossed luminosity,
like miller-moths thrilled
to be illumed and shadow-
free: we think of Artemis
and her Grecian bow, bent
wise and unneutered
by the night.

In the poem "Match," Gutteridge photographs life as it comes. He depicts life the way it happens – and it can happen to anyone. Down-to-earth occurrences that send even the consecrated ones into doubting: ("The Reverend Bell") "wondering… whether God was on his side." Job, the biblical character, comes to the picture ("Why have you made me your target?" "Have I become a burden to you?") *(Taken from Holy Bible, 1984, Zondervan Publishing House. Job's words in Job 7:20).* However, it is implicit that Gutteridge presents facts and narrates them for the reader to ponder, but also to smile. Let's enjoy this:

> *The Reverend Bell came home*
> *one afternoon, flung*
> *his cellar door wide*
> *and, though less than wise,*
> *lit a match: we found him*
> *sitting in a singed patch*
> *of his grass: surprised,*
> *a touch unhinged,*
> *and wondering how such*
> *things come to pass*
> *and whether God was on*
> *his side.*

My father smoked a pipe and long cigars when I was a little boy. He quit many years ago, more than forty-five, but I still remember the aroma of cigar and smoke and I still keep a wooden box where he placed his cigars. It is deeply registered in my emotional memories. "Helm" made me remember how essential scent (or sound) is for people. In reading "a lozenge of elm or oak" I instantly smelled wood scents coming from a carpenter's work-shop, and I was transported back in time. Gutteridge then blends scents with sounds: "through the burr and bite of the band-saw." There is a floating sense of onomatopoeic echoes, direct and indirect, in the combination of the sound "b" in "burr… bite… band."

Alliteration escorts the scene: "a particle of the puzzle he was perfecting piece by filigreed piece." I could not help noticing a gentle balance between the heavy work carried out in a work-shop: noise, sawdust, probably the logical mess of a place like that, and the child's full involvement ("I nuzzled in closer") with his grandfather's work, finely ended with "knowing I would be cherished and thrive here with this man at the helm" and preceded by "the unspoken tousling of my cowlick." It was a heart-caressing memory where the poet does not remember his exact age; but he does remember wood names!

An indelible experience, voiced in his bio: "I spent a lot of time in my grandfather's workshop, and adored him." Enjoy the poem:

> *I might have been five*
> *when I first wandered into*
> *my grandfather's workshop, and watched the hands*

I loved guide a lozenge
of elm or oak through the burr
and bite of the band-saw,
a particle of the puzzle he was perfecting
piece by filigreed piece,
and I nuzzled in closer,
waiting, in my need, for the pause
that preceded the unspoken
tousling of my cowlick,
and knowing I would be cherished
and thrive here with this
man at the helm.

Gutteridge serves us fond memories in "Apostasy." Feelings and human values are kindled in the furnace of human connection. From there emerge convictions and attitudes for life. Gutteridge praises his grandmother for her devoted undertaking of pie preparing and baking. As I read, I feel like I am right there watching her. The poem:

My grandmother baked
pies on Sunday mornings
(cherry, and rhubarb
in season, raisin for my
Grandpa's bucket), an echo
away from the Anglican nave
and apse she had no
reason to give the nod
of approval to nor taste
its soothing pieties, for she put
all of her love and outsized ardor into the gentle
kneading of her dough and braving
the wrath of a hairy-jawed
God, while we feasted
on her pastries and praised the Lord

Gutteridge relives two experiences: unique home-made food and religion. One is body-provider; the other, soul-provider.

"Rare" offers another touching memory for us, and awakens our own. Alliteration is present ("on the sand in his Sunday suit," "even dove under like daring dolphins"). Gutteridge leaves no memory/experience/anecdote in the darkness of forgetfulness. This time it is the beach, which most children adore. I understand the sensation of water, of being "perfectly safe" in the hands of my father, of "venturing up to our waists and even dove...," of "(he) smiled at us and we smiled back at him." Happiness is ripples, splashes and adventure in the beach.

A transition from innocence to an awakening from the "gender-free" games is reflected in "Chums." This is presented in the first stanza, as it dilutes into "– until the day." From that moment on, it was "I took a fancy to her burgeoning beauty." Don depicts falling in love, that first-time butterfly in the stomach and his acknowledging that he "felt my heart hum":

Nancy and I were chums,
playing our garrulous games,
gender-free, in Withers
field, festooned with sun-
light in the long summer
afternoons or under
Mara's lamp in the usurping
dark of Monck Street,
superintended by a marinating
moon—until the day
I took a fancy to her burgeoning
beauty and felt my heart
hum and a voice inside
singing Olly, Olly
en-fray.

"Abide" is another experience/anecdote illuminated by "a sun-stunned meadow." There is some rituality and solemnity to this particular day: "but there is this day no game to be got." The child admits the pleasure of the adult's company. The poet regales us with wonderful imagery: "our guns as silent as the thoughts we share." No need to talk, really, the "love that abides" keeps them connected.

My Uncle Potsy and I
go hunting cottontail
in a sun-stunned meadow,
and, if we are lucky, spot
a jackrabbit anteloping
speed in an open field,
but there is this day
no game to be got,
but all I need is striding
side by side with my uncle,
our guns as silent as the thoughts
we share, with a love that abides

Memories, experiences, stories are not always pleasant. So, Gutteridge wants to "redeem" himself by recalling that sad incident from years ago. He confesses that he "became something I was not: a bully." This poem, "Bully," is an I-am-sorry postcard to Susan.

The poet/viewer is enraptured by his surroundings in his poem "Dark": "we skated on glazed meadows." He remembers what and who was there, "clove bloomed," "wild mustard throve," "larks buffeted the air." The moon, so significantly recurring in Don's poems, cannot be left out of this scene: "amazing the moon as we moved…" Magnificent imagery to give us a landscape, one that Canadian poets are so good at describing, which Gutteridge uses to remember his school crush, Leckie:

When Leckie's field iced
over after a thaw
and quick freeze, we skated
on glazed meadows
where once clover bloomed,
wild mustard throve
and larks buffeted the air –
as if the globe had hewn
one raw rink
where we left in our wake
filigreed meridians,
mittened our hands in gendered
pairs, and unmuffled
our carnal cries – two
abreast lest we fall
off the world: amazing
the moon as we moved through
the lustrous rendering
of its light towards the star-
flecked obsidian dark.

A second title for the book could be the poem "Towards the Light." This poem does not mention the moon. There is no need for it: Mara's lamp is there instead. Gutteridge transported me to my 1970s childhood when my sister and I would cast hand-shadows, silhouetting from background candles, on the walls during power outage nights in my hometown…

While Don's poem reads about "nightfall," "dread of darkness," "inked shadows," he ends it with a clear passion and confidence of "knowing full well that, like every living thing, we all grow towards the light."

Nostalgia and remembrances come in "Together." How many times do we all go over our old family album? Those past days, those memories rekindled when we flip page after page – smiling, tears flooding our eyes, reliving them… I have a similar picture with my parents.

In this photo, my mother
and father, standing tall
on my grandfather's lawn
in their Sunday suits,
hold me up high
between them for the camera's
loving eye, like a prized
doll for all the world
to see, their hands tethered
to steady me on my maiden
shoot, as happy as they
will ever be, and I still
regret I wasn't enough
to keep them together.

"A Birthday Poem" is warm, intimate, sweet. The poet leans on love, "our abiding love." The line between brackets ("your hand in my glove") defines, for me, the mood of the poem. Together, poet and wife, Anne, "have eased into our age... gracefully." Notice the verb, "ease," which implies comfort, calm. That is how the poet sees their love and life together. A constant emphasis of the "we" and the "our": "We have stopped counting our birthdays… our say-so…" In the end, they have their ("our") "abiding love":

We have stopped counting
our birthdays, but the years
glide on without permission
or our say-so, but we have eased
into our age as gracefully
as Time and Earth allow
(your hand in my glove),
and whatever fears
we may have for the future
are flouted by our abiding love.

I have shared my views about some of the poems in *Home Ground.* In doing so, I have visited my own life, as I have been mirrored, so closely, in his poems. They have brought happiness and homesickness to my mind, and as Gutteridge himself expresses it in his last poem, "Defy," "poetry is both bliss and consolation, a way of speaking to the world that subsumes both shy and defy." He has spoken to the world. The world has replied: Erin Nichol Cochrane said, "… a poetry collection that will knock you off your boots in the sweetest of ways." Let's have "Defy" full:

For more than a dozen years
you were surrounded by blooms

in your shop, a long way
from Alberta's unlyrical
land, and when you tried
your hand at verse, were
your first poems for poppies
and their roaring red, sonnets
for sunflowers a-burst
in lavish light, haiku
for hibiscus and their passionate
purple, or pentameters
for peonies and their kissing cousins?
Did you let them speak?
for you, go soaring through the
petrified petal of your fear?
For poetry is both bliss
and consolation, a way of speaking
to the world that subsumes
both shy and defy.

Out of the Blue

Hidden Brook Press published more books by Gutteridge in 2019. *Out of the Blue* is a collection of his poems (selected by James Spence) from 1983 to 2011. About it, Erin Nicole Cochran was emotionally truthful, "It's only a handful of words but I felt this inside of me as though it were an epiphany of sorts. There is a classical instrumental quality to every poem…" and she finishes her comment, "Don Gutteridge's soul is on every page".

Some of his poems echo his earlier works and solemn style, like "Indian Summer: On a Farm Near Preston" and "Riel":

(excerpt from "Indian Summer")
… where stones have stood
a hundred autumns
and kept their true till spring,
and underneath the quiet earth
I hear November voices
singing of the deep fallow
where all the Indians lie.

(excerpt from "Riel")
There is no
eloquence to
blood running

from the mouths
of wounds and
battles lost,
the eyes
of the dead
at Duck Lake
and Batoche…
or will this
prairie be
a coffin
for my voice
a dwelling place
for
two
white
stones?

One particular piece I was fascinated by is "First Steps". We perceive innocence expressed with tender pen and candid heart fallen for an image of a toddler. We are pleasantly caught up in the sweet imagery and the soft touch pervading the whole poem. John Barnet shares this thought with us: "When Gutteridge turns to the subject of his grandchildren, his poetry is lovely and lyrical, and dances":

Your toes tingle the broad
pool of air and a leg
steps strident into its
smooth immensity,
the body follows with a feel
of floating,
then you grin
to let us know it's okay
to applaud.

The poem that entitles the collection, "Out of the Blue," is an ode of remembrance and optimism, of recognition of truth and unavoidable factuality but also of capacity to hold on to what is cherished:

Out of the blue a call
from a boyhood chum,
his name faintly stirring
at the edge of memory,
and quick as it's recovered
I am back in King
Edward Public School,

the years peeled away
as if they had never been,
and once again I am stunned
by the ease with which the past
obtrudes upon the present,
and nothing is ever lost:
not even the pain of what
we can never fully
regain.

Village Dreaming

Village Dreaming is another Hidden Brook Press 2019 publication. "Dunes at Canatara" (a poem I talked about when I reviewed *Point Taken*) is a *Purdian* gem as I commented then for its extolling voice to greatness before the human eye and feel:

It took a million years
to sculpt these dunes,
grain by grain of wave-
washed sand whipped
by seasoned winds into
voluptuous curves
and bevelled runes.
It took my pals and me
an afternoon to put
our imprimatur upon
the shimmering concavities,
our bodies pressing
their wry signatures deep
deep into the sun-stunned sand,
feeling the heat of a hundred
centuries oozing through.

Another superb piece is "Ruthless," a sustained chant to poetry, how a poet strives to pursue "the truth" and is fully engulfed by such "labor":
And me composing poems:

inklings I tease
towards some sense
in words whetted upon
the wheel of memory
and swerving askance

upon the page where they lean
upright, enlinked,
ready to be swallowed whole,
raw and ruthless
in rhythmic pursuit
of the truth.

"Au Revoir" is a heart-breaking poem. We see a sophisticated poet in love, deeply in love for his departed wife. Everything reminds him of her. Torn in pain and nostalgia, he weaves scene after scene, image after image, glued to the physicality of her memory. Despite grief – and/or fuelled by it – he manages to erect a monumental piece here and in other poems, "elegies for my beloved wife" as he told me:

I do not empty this house
of your presence: you are here
in every room we shared
breath in, your clothes still
hang where they belong
in their closets, and every painting
that adorns our walls is a reminder
of your artist's eye, and the chesterfield,
your bête noir, still
bears your imprint, and a novel
lies where your fingers last
lingered, nor am I made
forlorn on entering the space
now vacant of the woman
I cossetted and cradled with
love in its essence, for we are taught
that death is not an ending,
not goodbye but au revoir:
I refuse that platitude,
preferring your haunting hover
and the remnants of the things you touched
with such tenderness.

Inking the World

Also in 2019, Hidden Brook Press brings the reader *Inking the World*. The book's essence is superbly sketched in the opening piece, which entitles the book.

Whenever I think of my demise
I try to remember the day
my mother, still a girl,
unwombed me and I swallowed

a village whole and kept it
tucked inside the little
room of my mind for eighty-
one years, and I have grown
gracefully old and somewhat
wiser, embracing my age
and inking the world with poems.

"Be" engulfs the reader in nostalgia, illusion and cravings. The poet longs for what is gone, wants it back in his life yet channeling his thoughts into a possible tomorrow, into being "born again / in the place where I could merely / be." The verb BE acquires hues beyond a simple residence in space. It implies an existence in temporal terms, in physical terms that would allow him "to feel one more time / the brush of a breeze…"

I have such a longing
to see once again
the lush lavender of the lilacs
that hugged grandfather's lawn
and to feel one more time
the brush of a breeze combing
the leaves of our Manitoba maples
and to know the warmth of a home-
kitchen, love-tugged,
and to tingle with the touch of fingers
so tender I could dream
only of being in their embellished
embrace and I have such
a longing to be born again
in the place where I could merely
be.

The height in the book's general tenor is, in my view, "Blessed." Gutteridge summarizes how he feels in those classic words he has been able to forge during his poet's life. He is "blessed by fortune, / embossed by the gods, passionate / and true." Starting on a rhetorical question that is answered line after line, we walk with the poet's enumerations and "itemized" aspects of his long life besides his beloved Anne, to whom the poem is dedicated, finding shelter in beauty, love, truth, a rose, mementoes, being optimistic and objective in his understanding of life:

Does anybody know how deep
love goes or how radiant
a rose can be in the luminous
light of a June morning,

for we are born to love
and beauty, despite the odds,
and we suffer heartbreak
and loss like heroic stoics,
and I have known it all
since you first flowed
into view and we fashioned a life
together, blessed by fortune,
embossed by the gods, passionate
and true.

The book closes with "Village Dreaming," a poem included in *Point Taken*.

Rocking in my chair I dream
of the village where I was breathed
into being by the athletic lusts
of my hockey-heroing father
and the girl he deemed his paramour,
when my world was as new as a
chick picking at the shell
and a blank page I wrote
myself upon with words
wrestled from the womb, and a town
surrounded me with folks
to people my poems and startle
the stories I would create, in the
mortar and pestle of my imagination,
of their forgivable follies, the hustle
and bustle of their Dickensian lives,
and those childhood
chums I turned into combed
prose, who made my days
worth the telling and strummed
the strings of my memory, leaving
me to dream, rock and sing
the song of myself.

The Star-Brushed Horizon

Gutteridge's *The Star-Brushed Horizon* came out in 2019 as well. It must be read as a story, the poems within visualized as chapters. Each poem is a different yet strongly interconnected memory lane – interdependent synapses – the poet walks up and down in his rewarding recreation of characters, events, emotions and moments. Jack Magnus calls "these still breathing moments of memory." because they are alive in the poet's brain.

Allusions, people, places, names, echo back and forth, skip across the waters of a frequented pond, skate under a summer sky, or bask on a familiar beach. Gutteridge travels and takes us with him back in time, to a past that may well be our own pasts: his stories and ours will meet at many crossroads, coincide and link up these synapse-poems in our minds.

Emily-Jane Hills Orford stated: "Each one (poem) captures a precious moment, a cherished family member or friend, a glimpse of beauty in nature, in the skies, or at night and so much more." The general theme in the book moves from "… nature themed work to the memorial pieces celebrating friends and golfing companions…" From the first poem, "A Butterfly for Anne," we feel the light elegance of symbolism. The poet dedicates it to Gerry Parker, the actual muse being, as in so many wholehearted pieces, Gutteridge's Anne.

You send this exquisite
green butterfly in lieu of
a visit, perched poetically
on an amaze of lines,
alabaster moons and a dazzle
of dots fancied afresh:
a master's art that says
how much you loved my Anne,
that utters its grief through
its breathless beauty.

My eyes could not avoid noticing how often the poet employs a classic expressive means I have mentioned in this paper in earlier analyses, alliteration. It builds a melodic effect into the utterance and creates an emotional atmosphere, very much in line with the poet's state of mind and the poems' mood.

This is perceptible in many of his poems, a feature he referred to in his emails to me: "… my recent work (since 2012) is structured around internal rhyme, assonance and alliteration..." Notice it in "A Butterfly for Anne": "perched poetically," "dazzle of dots," "fancied afresh," "breathless beauty."

Cuban Apostle, José Martí, spoke highly of one of Cuba's 19th Century teachers, José de la Luz y Caballero, and his profession: "… he ambitioned nothing yet became everything, because he was a teacher…" Our next poem pays tribute, directly and gratefully, to teaching in the person of Ian Underhill, whom it is dedicated to (see the constant reference or allusions to family and friends). Underhill himself praised Gutteridge´s work too: "Don Gutteridge's new collection of poetry is, quite simply, outstanding… He leads us with breathtakingly alliterative phrases… into the very heart of his world and the heart of our own memories. This is a collection to be sipped slowly, like fine cognac, each poignant and physical moment treasured." The poem:

Purveyor
For Ian Underhill

You spent a lifetime
purveying poems and stories
to generations of students,
reading aloud with alliterative
ease in your sturdy baritone
until the rhymes chimed
and the consonants collaborated,
until the metaphors stood
up and mentioned their meaning:
you gave them Munro and Purdy,
Atwood and Lawrence,
and all you asked for in return
was their passionate attention
and some small acknowledgement
that teachers,, unglōried
as they are, really matter.

Achievements are condensed in three aspects, rhymes chimed, consonants collaborated, metaphors stood up and mentioned their meaning, and contribution concretized in the legacy of the names he calls as homage: "… you gave them Munro and Purdy, / Atwood and Lawrence…" Gutteridge's key statement comes at the end: "… all you asked for in return / was their passionate attention / and some small acknowledgement / that teachers, unglōried / as they are, really matter." The poem is an ode to a man that turns into an ode to teaching.

"Jury" stands as a mature understanding of life, philosophically approached, a happy reconciliation with what it has been and how it turned out for the poet. In between, an apt Shakespearean line, "I've had my day," and his effective pet tool, alliteration: "like a lark lifting," "last lick of light," "fuelled my fury." Here, the full poem:

It's been a long and satisfying
life, and I intend to go
gently into Dylan's Good
Night: after all,
I've had my day, weaned
my soul from strife and woe,

eased myself into age
like a lark lifting into air,
content with what has been
allotted me, but the jury's
still out: as the last lick
of light flickers in the dark,
I may shout "Nay!" – bent
by bravado, fuelled by fury.

We see what Jack Magnus termed as a "… world ostensibly simpler but so much richer…" *(ibidem, Magnus)* in "Reach." It is a piece where Don depicts simplicity and richness together; splendidness that feels exuberantly idyllic.

Read these lines, in which alliteration continues to amaze us (particularly in "we watched the wind-wafted waves"):

On sultry summer afternoons
we watched the wind-wafted
waves of Huron, as blue
as morning glories stroked
by lasering light, break
upon Canatara's
fabled beach, and we also
found time to cast
an unrighteous eye
upon the girls who once
were merely our chums
as they lay now full-
frontal on the sun-infused
sand, knowing all
along with our penultimate breath
that these creatures, lazing
there, feigning boredom,
would be forever beyond
our reach.

On the book's back cover, John B. Lee, in characterizing another Gutteridge book, *Home Ground,* refers to a recurring theme in the poet's work, "… the reader is presented with insight into the precocious child coming of age, engaged in imaginative play, experiencing the sexual stirrings of his gender…"

When we read "Fury," we understand universality in Gutteridge's poetics. It is a poem about the awakening of sexual interest, colorfully narrated, story-like. Even in the semantically vehement shades of the word fury, I imagine an "innocent fury," rather an energetic drive-in line with the intense emotions shooting through the young boys' brains.

How many summers did we while
away the days on Canatara
Beach, where the sun hummed
on the heat-soaked sand
and girls, new-breasted,
smile-beguiling and thigh-
shy, stretched out
before our salacious gaze
(hoping to be pursued perhaps),
but all we could do was shout
something rude
and plunge, unfazed, into Huron,
where we stroked each wave
with mammillary fury.

The rhetorical implication of the poem's first line, "How many summers did we while…" finds an "excuse" answer to reminisce, therefore, enumerate, play with original epithet-charged animate-inanimate references. I was amused by an interesting element in the last line, "mammillary fury."

The more common meaning of the attribute used by Gutteridge is "of or pertaining to a nipple, shaped like a nipple" *(Babylon English, Digital Dictionary)* yet according to the Concise Oxford English Dictionary, digital, the word has two more technical entries, one related to minerals, the other to anatomy, "denoting two rounded bodies in the floor of the hypothalamus in the brain." The hypothalamus is a region in the brain involved in emotional activity. This validates my previous remark about the energetic drive and intense emotions shooting through the young boys' brains.

However, we look at the poem and will invariably find peace, sound reminiscence and a realistic proposal resulting from the "studied attention in life to the past preserved in memory…" *(ibidem, John B. Lee)* Don's poetry grows memorializing, as I said, people, events, feelings, places – and pets. So is "Stranger," a piece written about a dog, Moochie, and about a kid, the poet, who is concerned about the dog's future. In quite an imaginative spin, the boy wonders, "what dog-thoughts / went whistling through his head…" attributing human qualities to the animal. Let me share the entire poem with you:

When our dog Moochie
fell ill with distemper,
my father drove him into the
countryside and dropped
him off, and I've always
wondered what dog-thoughts
went whistling through his head
as, confused, dazed,

abandoned, he started up
the nearest lane, hoping
some stranger would call
out, "Here, pooch!"
and show him more love
than we did.

Now read this poem,

Roan
For Grace Leckie

I watched you galloping
across the fallow field
on your stalwart stallion
with a thigh-gripping ease,
and waited while you went
coursing by, your hair
bountiful in the breeze,
the roan tight-lipped,
nostrils a-flare, and I wasn't
sure whether I loved you
more, or the horse.

We encounter plenty of examples of alliteration, hints of vim and movement to enhance scenic effects – galloping, fallow field (flat terrain that allows free rein), stalwart stallion, hair bountiful in the breeze, nostrils a-flare (suggesting breathlessness and speed) – and the end line closing with a touch of comedy the picture the poet has sketched in our heads.

This poem is a poetic urge emerging from Don's school days. He recalls it this way: "I became entranced by a grade 7 girl, Grace Leckie, who occasionally rode to school on a chestnut stallion…"

Moving along with memories, we come to the piece "Exalted." Reading the first two lines is enough to understand a man's allegiance to his love: "Loving you is an act / of remembrance." The poet might as well say "remembering you is an act of love," both expressions valid in his committed voice, in his dearest recollections. The poem is a "celebration of moments," as Magnus tells us *(ibidem, Magnus)*:

Loving you is an act
of remembrance, a recalling
of all those days when we were
too young to be tempered
by tactful touch or the soft
collision of lips, when being

amazed was our common fare,
when I knew such jolting
joy at a glimpse of your hair
haloed by juddering sun-
light or your eyes as blue
as crystallized cobalt
or the effortless allure
of your youthful gaze:
in truth our love was too
exalted to be nipped
in the bud.

Deeper into the book we find a biblically resounding poem, "Desire." It is a parable of sexual awakening, amusement and refocusing on emblematic themes in Gutteridge (also treated by other poets I have reviewed):

When God ripped Eve
out of Adam's ribs, what
he saw was a mirror image
of himself: with breasts
unsuckled and an extra
cleft and hair that hung
like flung flowers; he felt
no fire in his loins
as hand-in-hand they strolled
the groomed sod, until
Eve purloined an apple,
and Adam, smitten, came
unbuckled with desire.

The poet's supreme muse, Anne, lives in the following piece,

Loving You
For Anne
Loving you is as easy
as breathing, and our long
lives have not diminished
the intricate dance of our
separate selves,…

Intimately simple and revelatory of the mutually responsive inner bonds that sprout gently yet unbreakably out of an acknowledged "partnership" of two people who have loved each other. It is best worded by the poet as "the separate selves" in an "intricate dance." The closing lines, as the whole poem, are premium statements of love:

… and above
all else we touch
each other in ways
that have no need for
anything other than a
knowing nod or a con-
junctive squeeze
of the hand.

Thus we come to the end of the book with "Eventually" which is a hymn to the futility of things and life yet in calm, pensive tones reassuringly asking the reader to partake in the balance he has achieved, in the remembrance stage we all reach, eventually. The last two lines are an axiomatic fact of life.

When we were young and easy
in our own skin, we let
our bodies be as they pleased,
happy to find a home
in one another's arms,
and as we grew wiser
we met thigh to thigh
and our love sprung anew
with each familiar sigh,
and when age surprised
us out of the blue,
we let ourselves be
content to sit side by side
in abiding repose, knowing
that everything kith
and kin eventually goes.

Finally, "Pendulum" closes a book with five stars in its horizon. It is a superb piece where the poet challenges the old saying, "You know what you've got only when it's gone." Gutteridge knew since day one what he had, and beautifully admits it in this poem. Imagery fills its lines from the very beginning, as the poet likens his grief to a pendulum and his pain both subsides and surges back as he looks at the things that are monuments of remembrance, a yellow rose, the chesterfield, the halls. Let's have the poem,

My grief, like a pendulum,
comes and goes, the sight
of a yellow rose, emblem
of our long loving years,

can overwhelm or the chesterfield
where you lay during your last
days can amaze tears
I had thought forgotten,
but mostly it is the ghost
haunting these halls
above and below, but it's good
to mourn what we have lost,
for it tells us how far
love has come.

Point Taken

Point Taken (Hidden Brook Press, 2019), a huge, 600 page, 7 X 10 inch, welcome undertaking, puts together most of Gutteridge's previous work. I must say that those early years in his life when he was "consuming the small library there (at Point Edward and nearby township) and writing both his first poem and his only play", were such a strong influence for his career, and a reminder of my own childhood.

Those were actually career-defining moments: "… he spent his first eleven years in a childhood enlivened by schoolyard chums and summers spent sunning on Canatara beach and paddling in the chill waters of Lake Huron… pristine days of his boyhood… There he spent three idyllic years…" that furnished Don's budding formative period and left marks on what would be his exceptional style and ability to recreate the past and lay it down freshly, strikingly and kindheartedly. It also built a foundation for his gallant, brave and confident attitude towards today and his being at peace with tomorrow.

This book has the rare touch to make me travel. While on my spatial-temporal voyage, I have been led into my own soul, my own memories, dusting many of them out of an almost forgotten past. I thank Gutteridge for it.

It unveiled gently, completely, a universe of shimmering words and images to replenish the soul. Jack Magnus tells us of Don's craft "in making his images sing…"

The book is divided into self-standing yet mutually-cohesive titles and dates that feel like sections, hand-guiding the reader across its over seven hundred pages. Despite its length, Gutteridge has succeeded in collecting poems that will stay with us long after we have finished the book. John B. Lee tells us about Gutteridge and his poetry: "we might carry these poems with us where we go…" We will put the book down with a mixture of states and feelings wafting about us. We will feel a bit of fatigue from the long, edifying journey, but also a generous pinch of satisfaction for being witnesses to the extensive high-polish oeuvre the author has compiled throughout his prolific writing career, magnificently displayed here. We will be proud for sharing in the message and scope of his work, sincere acknowledgement to the merits of the book and the poet, and a sense of belonging to that group of people who are now in possession of an extraordinary volume.

On *Home Ground*'s back cover too, Jack Magnus's impressions about the poet's work cannot be more commendable: "… instilled in me a sense of wonder and presence at his memories…" and he goes on to say: "the reader can't help but be affected."

In my view, this book is to be approached with spirit and an open will to walk down the roads Gutteridge paves for us. You will need time, which you can profit from alone, or in the company of beloved ones. The poems in the book are heartening, inviting and embracing. John B. Lee best coincides about the effect of poetry when he says: "kissing the darkness / when the pages are closed / and silent / as a dreamer's mind…" *(Taken from Lee's poem "Kissing the Darkness When the Pages Close")*

The book gives us a latent past, a defining present and a future that may well be anyone's future. That is how I felt regarding this book and its lingering aroma after reading it. The book's parts are The Way it Was, Tidings, Peripheries, Inundations, The Blue Flow Below, The Sands of Canatara, Inklings, Cameron Lake: a Suite of Poems, Home Ground, Night Skating, Days Worth the Telling, The Breath of My Being, The Star-Brushed Horizon, Foster's Pond, Mara's Lamp and Inking the World.

A review of this intense-extensive compendium of colorfully-varied images and aesthetically-carved proposals must attempt at revealing its straight-to-the-heart poetic vision and stylistic precision, masterfully evidenced by the poet. To this end, I will make reference to some of the poems in some of the sections. It will help me illustrate my analyses and clarify my criteria for the readers.

Gutteridge presents his formidable book in a chronological arrangement of his literary production, 2014 through 2019, fanning out his most intimate nexus with syllable, word, rock-solid meanings and indelible metaphors, which are finely expressed in his poem for John B. Lee in *Home Ground*:

Syllables
For John B. Lee
We started a conversation
about poems and their making,
about the inheld breath
before we say the syllables
to ourselves and dream
them onto the page,
willing some meaning
that seems beyond knowing,
some home-truth
that needs no proof
to startle the world we build
together in a friendship
welded by words.

In The Way It Was section, the author embarks on a trip to his early reminiscences, and he gives us a free ticket to follow him. His poem "Blue-eyed," for example, abounds in tender phrases that depict moments and scenes familiar to everyone, thus creating links that we cannot break (full):

For my Grandmother: 1888-1957
My grandmother: shaking
dust-bunnies out of her mop
in a willing wind, and me,
at five, hopping in a one-
footed dance at her side,
the serene sun alive
in her hair as together
we breathe easy in the April
air, crisp clouds
clustered above: her glance
a blue-eyed barometer
of her love.

The two instances settle comfortably in our mind's innermost recesses, playfully activating our personal experiences, positively connecting us to this and the next pieces. "Letters" follows up in the trail of the previous poem. Earnest lines worth quoting for the reader, where Gutteridge displays his seasoned skills to give us his grandfather:

For my Grandfather: 1892-1955
I am now the last one
who will remember my grandfather, and so it is
I try again to catch
that fleeting face in the prism
of a poem, to see it
again with the clarity of crystal
and feel that benign smile
in the serendipity of a simile,
knowing that he will survive
as long as these letters
linger and thrive.

I could not avoid recalling Shakespeare's "When in eternal lines to Time thou grow'st." "Dunes at Canatara" shows us a poet of deep thought, of concerned meditation about time and land, which he gracefully blends with his own life. The poet does not detach himself from the land; he rather admires such creation and paints himself, and peers, into it:

It took a million years
to sculpt these dunes,

grain by grain of wave-
washed sand whipped
by seasoned winds into
voluptuous curves
and bevelled runes.
It took my pals and me
an afternoon to put
our imprimatur upon
the shimmering concavities,
our bodies pressing
their wry signatures deep
deep into the sun-stunned sand,
feeling the heat of a hundred
centuries oozing through.

I pick Purdy echoes in this poem: "I lay with my ear flat against the monstrous stone silence…, listening to the deep core of the world – silence unending and elemental, leaked from a billion-year period before and after the season of man." *(Fragment by Al Purdy in Al Purdy. Essays on his Works, essay by Stan Dragland)*
We enjoy sound humor in "Career":

Oscar and I boxing
in the home-built ring
suddenly my chin…
too close to the gist
of Oscar's toxic fist,
and down I go, sprawled
on the cellar floor, knocked
here and everywhere
at once, and contemplating
the demise of my illustrious
career.

We smile in half-closed-eyes gratefulness with "Nightfall" as we roll back to our childhood:

When night came down
upon the village verge,
we gathered around
the intergalactic glow
of the streetlight like
marauding moths, and it
was hide-and-go-seek,
as, in our pulsing panic,
we combed every ell

and alley to burrow in;
then ululating ally-
ally-in-free, we
rocketed out of
our hiding holes, triumphant,
until something
darker than night called
us ineluctably
home.

In the section Tidings I was deeply moved by "The Way Home":

The way home is thru
the heart, every blood-
beat hums with remembrance,
the village at the nub
of our being runs deep,
keeps our aloneness
at bay wherever
it finds us: estranged
as we are and listening
hard for that
emphatic thrum.

This is a recurring leitmotif in Gutteridge, sweetly handled and firmly setting in our minds. Then again in "Home-grown" those Purdy vibrations that speak of the land, how Gutteridge mentions places of special connotation during his growth:

… the curve of Canatara's bountiful beach,
the infinite surge
of Huron Lake, the marshes
below the angular Bridge
spanning the blue
cadence of our River,
while meadows bounced
with bobolinks near a park
where we played until
the evening evaporated
– these were all of God's
geography I would need
to track the terrain of a story
or the swerve of a poem
with my cartographer's eye…

This is continually singularized in the poems "The Lake of my Childhood" and "Pleasure." One particular poem of endearment is "For my Grandmother." He had dedicated a previous one I presented above. This poem reaffirms Magnus's axiom: readers will be affected by Gutteridge's words.

When grandfather died
your world was abruptly halved,
all those little rituals
that bound you one to one
now ended, you could not bear
ever again to sleep
in the bed you shared for more
than fifty years, your dreams
entangled through the long night
until morning woke you
with a new day; I remember
you best in the evenings,
you knitting in the kitchen,
Gramps snoozing through the news
a room away, but both of you
linked by love.

The axiom applies also in "Allies":

Nothing abides like love:
for fifty-odd years
side by side we have
weathered the world and not
grown weary, two
souls allied as one
since that moment so
long ago when we eyed
one another and satisfied
something wistful
inside; and here, now,
riding out our last days,
we smile and, knowingly,
nod.

These lines confirm my assertion about the poet's attitude in regards to what is ahead, his confidence and mature stance. He portrays his life poem after poem, his family, his fears and joys; and we gently ease into them and feel on our skin what he has felt. Peripheries is a section of little jewels as well. "Letters" speaks about the emotions stirred inside the poet. He enumerates them slowly, as if to imbue all the homesickness they inspire, as if to relive the past that now passes before his eyes:

It's a long way home
to the place where the heart lies:
the village that superintended
my birth, that gave me space
in its eyes to grow under
its lavish light...
a place where the heart lives,
etched in perpetual Spring,
unravished by Time.

The last line tells us of the durable tie between poet and place. Gutteridge is loyal to the Canadian tradition of writing about nature and the elements. In his poem "Gloaming" he impresses us with a splendid, eye-caressing feat of images, similes and metaphors:

On soft autumn evenings
we would play move-up
in the field behind Wiz's
with a half-strung ball
that sizzled when struck
by the cracked bat and floated
like a drunken dolphin till
someone, lad or lass,
interrupted its flight
and it fizzled in the dew-limn'd
grass a long way
from home-plate, as the dark
deftly descended and the moon
lurked aloft, a-glimmer
in the gloaming.

This is equally valid for "Eternity," a brief, passionate and nostalgic poem I quote fully:

My Lake was bigger than the
salten seas with no
horizon but a blue blur
where the sun would sequester
each evening, with a
kaleidoscopic squeeze,

and when we dipped a toe
into its chilled solemnity
and felt its heavenly breeze
upon our chastened cheeks,
it was is if we were touching
Eternity.

I praise the poet for his delicate, well-outlined images and epithets: "kaleidoscopic squeeze," chilled solemnity," "heavenly breeze," "as if we were touching Eternity."

"Unsayable" closes this part with the poet's musings about poetry writing. John B. Lee seeks answers to the mystery of writing: "… to feel the fertile germination / of a sentient breath / transforming / tight-packed syllables / of interlocking words…" (*"Kissing the Darkness When the Pages Close")* whereas Gutteridge explores possibilities and offers explanations:

I've spent a lifetime
seeking the reason for rhyme
in pursuit of the perfect poem
where dactyls dance until
they make indelible sense
in the midst of metrical meaning,
where I find my heart stirred
by the motive for metaphor
in the ept uttering of the un-
word, the saying of what is,
alas, unsayable.

He does not give up ("I've spent a lifetime") and certainly does persist in the act, "in pursuit of the perfect poem," while his metaphors waltz: "where dactyls dance…"
Yet, "Silence" epitomizes this quest towards the why and the mystery of writing:

For sixty-odd years
I've been a wielder of words,
my pen propelled across
the page, metamorphosing
into three-beat iambics
enmeshed in metaphor
and circulating into sense;
when I can no longer be
a purveyor of poems,
I shall leave it all
to God and silence.

We see the deeply religious man, poised and assured. Few poets spend so much time and sculpt such excellent pieces of poetry in dealing with this topic, and few achieve such heights in their attempts.

Inundations is a section that recaptures the scenes the poet so adores: family, context and childhood memories, sprinkling these with poems to nature, seasons, places and experiences like falling in love. Seasons, for instance, reverberate miraculously in his "Dappled":

When I die I want
it to be in the Spring
when the crocus erupts,
tulips tantalize
the sun, my maple's
leafage abruptly
levitates and the hedgerows
are hung with berries ripened
by light, when apple blossoms
blow blizzard-white,
and I may lie in some
dappled shade and dream
of being young.

A sense of belonging and a bond with nature are noticeable in this poem, as much as in "Birdsong" – and many others. The notion of poetry writing is revisited by Gutteridge in this section too. Here we find "Wit":

Once more I sit
down to compose,
amazed again at the
limned linkage
between the ink-dark
word and the flush of feeling
induced – the pivot-point
in the poem's truce with truth,
where the reader embarks
on a voyage that will leave him
dazed with knowing: words
are both weapon and wit.

"The Game"
I'd like to write a poem
to take your breath away,
but words have a will of their own:

once uttered indelible
into the air they will have their say,
and when they are stilled on the page,
stiff and resolute, they may
be read in a dozen different
ways or, playing the guessing
game, remain un-
engaged or merely mute.

"Rhymes"
In my advancing age
let me still be the one
wrestling with words to wield
the world anew, to send
them dancing on some
distant dais, sylvan
with simile: the page
where all my rhymes ring
true. with simile: the page
where all my rhymes ring
true.

Shakespeare's line "All my best is dressing old words new" echoes magnificently in Don's "Rhymes": "wrestling with words to wield / the world anew." In the modesty the poets show, we realize how concerned they are with the continuity of what they write. In Don it explains the role he wants to keep investing his words with, a fight to effect change around him.

The Blue Flow Below, The Sands of Canatara, Inklings, Cameron Lake: a Suite of Poems, Home Ground, Night Skating, Days Worth the Telling, The Breath of My Being, The Star-Brushed Horizon, Foster's Pond, Mara's Lamp and Inking the World will show the reader a Gutteridge nurtured by his past, charmed by his present, and in concord with what the future holds for him. This notion is visible in my next analyses. I especially remarked that in *Star-Brushed Horizon.* Don's penmanship can be explored further in my detailed analysis of *Home Ground*, available in the above pages.

I have gone back on my own life, as I have been mirrored, so closely, in Gutteridge's *Point Taken.* His collection of poems has brought happiness and homesickness to my mind. Even when Point was taken, it was I, reader and admirer, taken too into the glorious poetic knitting Gutteridge has done for us in this book. About it, K. C. Finn said, "… it's fair to say that there is something for everyone amongst the many themes and influences of the poet's life… a powerfully penned collection of sentiment, nostalgia, emotion, and observation… I really enjoyed the theme of capturing memories that will last long after us and recording moments and people from the past."

K. C. Finn's words help us grasp the book's worth: "Don Gutteridge writes most of his verses in a similar style of rhythm and pacing, which offers a kind of comfort to readers as you begin to feel that flow and pacing of his words in a very natural way. I really enjoyed the theme of capturing memories that will last long after us and recording moments and people from the past. It gave many of the works the feel of a loving tribute and a recreation of a glorious past for us to step into for a moment. What results is a powerfully penned collection of sentiment, nostalgia, emotion, and observation that takes a traditional look at verse in the best possible way. Every poem you pick from this collection feels like an instant classic, and overall, I would highly recommend *Point Taken: Collected Poems 2014 – 2020* for poetry fans looking for a deep and meaningful collection."

Christian Sia says: "These poems are filled with the humanity of the writer and readers can easily relate to the emotions evoked in the lines… While the collection features poems written over a span of six years, they explore recurrent themes like life and love, family, nature, humanity, the meaning of death, and many others. Each poem reads well, each has hidden importance, a unique meaning. The work is filled with vivid imagery, from the elements of nature to strong feelings inspired by genuine human contact and thoughts on reality.

Imagery and music play a key role in poetry. Poet Becky D. Alexander enthusiastically explains it: "Our teacher, after each recitation, would talk about how imagery worked and how in reciting poetry your voice should reflect and infuse the words with its music and emotion. She had me hooked. I loved the flow of poetry's lines, the way words could paint scenes and convey how you felt…" *(IN a paper written by James Deahl)*

Alexander´s words apply to Don Gutteridge, who writes in a style where imagery and music elevate his resulting pieces. His poems are a powerful testament of both the poet's impressive technique and musicality and his awareness of life within and around him.

As he hoped in his poem "Eternity," I can state Don has been able to memorialize his life in this book and leave for us a recorded legacy, thus touching eternity. His books are poetry and autobiography. They reach out to people and remind them of their own lives. Shrabastee Chakraborty says it best: "I can truthfully say that reading this book has enriched me. I heartily recommend it to any reader who appreciates poetry or simply loves looking back on a life well-spent."

Point Taken is the book of books of Don Gutteridge. It should be among the top recent poetry books a reader must have and hold, go to for inspiration, for enlightenment, for pleasure, for the sheer elation of reuniting in time and space with family, friends, remembrances, then place it back on a treasure-keeping bookshelf feeling complete, always willing to return to the book for feedback and spiritual enrichment.

Invincible Ink

Thus we come to 2020 with another Hidden Brook Press publication, Don Gutteridge's *Invincible Ink*. This is a 111-poem volume loyal to the themes and style that have made Gutteridge one of the best poets in the Canadian "poetdom."

The first poem, "Litmus," honors the craft of composing a poem. The poet states fluently and tastefully what poetry writing is about. I do not see an attempt to limit its definition; it is rather a preamble, comprehensive one, to what each individual may feel. It gives us open territory to roam free after "the brink of begetting." Nonetheless, there is a statement in the poem which may well be a definitive reference when it comes to declaring the urges, aesthetics and boundless realms of poetry, "for a poem, ancient / or newly honed, is really / a surging of the soul towards / the litmus of light or the mind." These are epigrammatic lines. Whatever we pursue poetically can be sparked by reading them. Let's enjoy the whole piece:

The urge to pen a poem
is as old as the lullaby sung
to ease the sleep of a fretting
child or the heartfelt hymn
to an ungrateful god or a
soliciting psalm to the setting
sun, for a poem, ancient
or newly honed, is really
a surging of the soul towards
the litmus of light or the mind
on the brink of begetting: words
stirred afoot, seasoned
with invincible ink.

Nature will never part from Canadian poets. The next poem I present bathes in it, finds nourishment in beauty and the cycle of seasons, motifs we discern in all five gems I have discussed in this book. "Wintering" is a seasonal passage as the poet moves slowly, in detail, across seasons.

Nothing escapes him. Even in the leaf's grief, "Bereaved of its leaves, this / maple in my fallen yard / stares bare-boned / into a sky," Gutteridge acknowledges the power of nature, of the earth's renovating magic. This faith can only endure in the poet's reassurance of life's constant renewal:

Bereaved of its leaves, this
maple in my fallen yard
stares bare-boned
into a sky, clotted with cloud
in the wilting light from a sun
bereft of its summer heft,
and in this time
of fallowed fields and the fringing
of frosts, we trust in the Earth's
rebirth, when bulbs bulge

with soon-to-be blooms
and robins throb with the nurturing
need and April rains
seize the sleeping seed
and waken it whole to the world,
but it is come Autumn now
and, ever a sinner, I must
winter over my soul.

The same feeling pulsates in "Wings," the poet's necessary shelter in tomorrow:

Outside my window
the trees are de-leafing,
there is an autumnal hum
to the wind and all things
summer come undone,
and though I have no heart
for what Winter brings,
I remain steadfast
in my belief that Spring will glide
into bloom on welcoming wings.

The elegance and tenderness we enjoy in Gutteridge's heartfelt poems overwhelms us when we read "Furious Felicity." The title hints two expressive means of the language, alliteration and oxymoron. Gutteridge has been showing his skilled use of these and other means throughout his work. The repetition of the consonant "f" echoes classic poems of yore (Poe's "The Raven," for example: "For the rare and radiant maiden…" the "r" recurrence).

But the title also carries a basic opposition of meaning between the noun modifier, "Furious," and the noun "Felicity." This semantic-stylistic clash is noticeable in the poem's mood. Above all, we sigh with the profound sensitivity and dripping melancholy the poet words in his oniric dialogue with his beloved one.

While we perceive grief and bits of irony, they never outshine the intimacy and love flowing across the lines. Let's have this heart-touching piece full here to close my comments:

I wake in your arms once
again, unforsaken,
and even though I know
I'm dreaming, I hug you
like the last Adam in Eden
offering Eve a paradisal
pass to the celibate sun,
and I want to tell you

there are gods that keep us
from harm's way, from being
a delegate to Death, and that love
with its furious felicity redeems
us all, but that would be
a luxurious lie, for such
deities let me love
and you, die.

As I said in my final words about *Point Taken*, for feedback and spirituality we must always go to the classics. Don Gutteridge is one of them. I have been on a long voyage across his poetic ocean, my life illuminated by this glistening Canadian gem, yet there is still much more.

Those fortunate to read most of Don Gutteridge´s oeuvre, do realize how loyal he is to memories, characters, names of people and places, all of which have shaped his poetic patrimony and given it a notable foothold into posterity. This is a tradition firmly rooted in the beginnings of Canadian literature, as Northrop Frye observed, "metaphoric mappings of peoples and places became central to the evolution of the Canadian literary imagination…" *(Taken from https://www.britannica.com/biography/Anne-Michaels, article written by Kathy Mezei)*

Lilacs in Lavender Light

In reading *Lilacs in Lavender Light*, another 2020 Hidden Brook Press publication, I re-comprehended the poet´s scope, his artistry and evident gratefulness in revisiting his dearest recollections of a life filled with events, family, friends, locations that fulfilled his aspirations and served a two-way function: they conformed the key ingredient of his vast work, which in return granted Gutteridge a niche of privilege in Canadian literature. His themes have populated his poems endowing them with vitality, tenderness, real-life instances that remain with the readers long after they finish one of his many books.

Lilacs in Lavender Light gratifies us for its adherence to those principles of writing Gutteridge has brilliantly sustained and developed as a master of his craft. Nature, narrated with keen insight and easy-going account, bursts before the readers´ eyes in the poem, "Time´s Tick." The poet blends human characters with bustling life he skillfully "photographs":

… passing Leckie's farm where Holsteins
graze lazily and shorthorns
remember themselves
and on past Gunn's place
where hogs wallow like hippos
with snouts in the snuffling mud
and the pasture where Grace grips
her stallion with incising thighs…

Alongside, splendid expressive means greet our eyes: epithets, like "sun-strummed September" or onomatopoeic rings in "titillating / Time's tick." The scenes are presented by the poet in pulsing "footage," as if his eyes were a camera panning the vista and recording them. Below, the poem:

On a sun-strummed September
morning we abandon our summer
cocoons and hit the high
road for school, passing
Leckie's farm where Holsteins
graze lazily and shorthorns
remember themselves
and on past Gunn's place
where hogs wallow like hippos
with snouts in the snuffling mud
and the pasture where Grace grips
her stallion with incising thighs
and the hawthorn hedge where this
year's colt burgeons
his brand-new erection
(and the girls blush lushly
and the boys sing inside)
and in the haze ahead
sits the brick-coat
box we will inhabit
until the sprouting of Spring
releases us and I shout
for the sheer joy of titillating
Time's tick.

Gutteridge handles the poem "Chum" with an able hand. Adolescence emerging, a boy´s first steps into it and the revelations that follow, thread this piece with bits of humor, plays on word meanings (piece, sweet); but above all with a natural depiction of the onrush of love and sex:

When Marilyn, my chum from school,
in the first bloom of her girl-
hood (with curls as wisped
as winter wheat), sauntered
past the hired hand
and me, the latter thumbed
his crotch, grinned and said,
"Now ain't that a sweet piece!"

and I wondered what part
of her he meant and what
made it sweet.

Our next poem reminds me (it is my strong contention readers must see this – and all themes – as an element of linking cohesion in Gutteridge´s storylines) of a piece in *Into the Milkweed Meadow* (Hidden Brook Press, 2021), a book analyzed later in this book, entitled "True." With *Lilacs in Lavender Light* Gutteridge continues his exploration of that "story" with his poem "Legacy," where Miss Bray remains a core motif in his writing (many poems are about her, like "Greening").

Alliterative echoes are felt in the poem, "roses as red / as a bride's blush," "lush as lavender" (his book´s title is *Lilacs in Lavender Light,* an obvious sound pattern), "pulsing with pollen," "do their dizzying dance," etc.

More focused this time on Miss Bray´s magnetic surroundings, the poet reinforces her aloneness with "The widow Bray stands / there alone, bee- / deep in her tenderly-groomed / garden…" From that line on, we witness a plethora of colors, activity, movement where she finds relief from "the legacy of her loss." The context is her savior; she finds solace in tending her garden. Here, the poem:

The widow Bray stands
there alone, bee-
deep in her tenderly-groomed
garden (with poppies bleeding
scarlet, roses as red
as a bride's blush and violets
as lush as lavender), watches
the drones, pulsing with pollen,
do their dizzying dance
to apprise the hive of her blossoms'
whereabouts, and thrives
in her flowered bower like a
bloom-inducing wizard
despite the legacy of her loss.

From a recent study I made of John B. Lee´s poetry (an essay book, *Five Canadian Poets*, where Don was also included together with Glen Sorestad, James Deahl and A. F. Moritz) I derived other analyses (work in progress) positing that "there are poems that relate to our lives and worldview more significantly than others, or touch differently our innermost niches of emotion." I share this idea because my next Don poem enters the categories of relatedness, significance and emotion.

"Bonding," an evocative title, is about Don´s experiences with his father. I have written about my family too, especially father and mother (for whom Gutteridge regales us "Contemplation"), so I instantly connected with this piece. The learning curve we all have as we grow and the memories we build along the way are mostly linked to events like the one narrated in "Bonding."

Fast-paced, as hunting may be, suspenseful, hectic and promising, the poem walks us down a trail of potential preys father and son follow. Gutteridge does not give up his creativity linguistically speaking and offers us metaphorical feats like "the afternoon / wears softly on in hopes…" as he puts layer after layer of adrenaline in the poem and the readers. The poem is an ode to those moments when we set deeper nexuses with our family. Between the lines, the tender dénouement in the boy´s words, as he misses the shot. Below, the poem:

My father and I go hunting,
twelve gauges slung
over our arms, ambling
side by side, kicking
at every brush-pile
and bramble bush as the afternoon
wears softly on in hopes
that some prey would startle
and there was no need
for the warmth of words until
a cottontail leaps out
and zigzags away;
"Fire!" and I do, wincing
at the rough recoil, but the rabbit
keeps running and Dad says,
"It's only a rabbit," and I say,
"I'm glad I missed."

Another poem that follows wonderfully this father-son aspect is "That´s How it´s Done." The closing words, told by the kid – Gutteridge – in the poem summarizes its mood and value for the poet, "and I wish the day would last / forever" (A line that is repeated in his poem "Wish", or a general urge picked in "Waddle," for example). Let´s have the whole piece:

My Dad and I fishing
on Mitchell's Bay, and I watch
in awe at the lazy, lofted
loop of his plug and its soft
plop on the weed-rich
shallow and when a pike
as big as a barnacled barracuda
strikes, he sets the hook

with an infinitesimal tug
and waits for the finned wriggler
to break the surface, its muscling
arc bent like Robin's *bow,*
defying the grasp of gravity,
but the fight is over, the game
won, and my father grins
at me as if to say,
'That's how it's done!"
and I wish the day would last
forever.

Following on the theme of family, I present here the poem I mentioned, "Contemplation," written by Gutteridge to his mother:

You tell me you found your mother
cold to the touch, the morning
sun pouring golden
upon the shimmered sheets,
and you but a girl of thirteen,
contemplating death and all
it means and not knowing
of course that I would discover
my own mother without breath,
feigning sleep, and I longed
to feel you warm once
more, your eyes smitten
with a smile, but we are all
hostage to love and loss, to laughter
at our a-borning and weeping at our demise

Romantic, reminiscent, great is our next poem, "Long-Ago." Gutteridge reexamines his younger years and his passage through life. There is admirable imagery, "I remember… / my youth, when every morning / was a rebirth and we were like / butterflies fluttering free…" or "the blue / embrace of Lake and River / and First Bush where the celibate / sun rose righteous / and I ambled iambic…" Above all, we read of the poet´s affair with poetry and its musicality. The final two lines are first-class evidence of what writing has meant for Gutteridge. The poem:

I remember the long-ago days
of my youth, when every morning
was a rebirth and we were like
butterflies fluttering free

from their wombed cocoons
in the lucid air over
grandfather's lilac hedge
blooming voluminous and we had
no brink but the blue
embrace of Lake and River
and First Bush where the celibate
sun rose righteous
and I ambled iambic, past
Mara's lamp on is pilgrim
pole, prefacing poems
as I went, to the water's edge,
where I dipped my pen in Ink
Lake and wrote myself whole.

"The Seasons as They Come" is one of the pieces included in the book´s section *SEVEN FOR ANNE in loving memory*. Pained in his loss, the poet exposes his feelings, likening his personal state of mind to nature, *the* motif, *the* poem-prompter par excellence. In the end, the man holds on to, and thanks for, the beauty of what they had, the meaning of their love, and the inevitable, supreme need to "carry on." The poem:

Now that you are gone
summer skies are not
so blue, the demise of autumn's
leaves is more subdued,
winter's snow sifts
less softly and the bulb-burst
of spring brings no
relief from my bereavement pain,
and so it is I face
the seasons as they come, hold
aloft our having loved,
acknowledge the gift of your grace
and carry on.

His feelings for Anne continue to fill us in "Lament," or "Adieu," where Don redresses words, crafts them anew like a Shakespeare, fights his loneliness, and leaves with us this heart-moving poem:

Lament
I wake and feel the luff
of the dark and when I reach
for you, you are gone and I am

alone in a bed big
enough for two, and our love
like a star fixed in the firmament
or a candle with twin wicks
still burns anew,
and I try not to feel forsaken

Adieu
In the midst of my grieving
I forgive you your leaving,
for ours was a love rooted
in passion that mellowed with the years
like a June moon and we grew
in unison like the rings of a slow
oak and I am comforted
at the last by the memories that linger
and loll and by the stalwart
sting of my tears as I bid you
adieu.

Later in the book I came across other moving poems written to Anne, "Touch," "In the Bone" and "Alight." The intimate dialogues knit by Gutteridge with this wife are sweetly provoking, passionate, unique. "Touch" is one of the most tender pieces to be found in the book – and there are many of these… The poem:

We lie in the lee of the dark
and let moonlight flow
molten over us, and thigh
to thigh we tingle with touch,
and I want so much to hold you
till doomsday dawns,
to watch your bedizening eyes
open to me like a slow-
blooming rose, to canonize you
whole and feel you singing
in my soul.

"In the Bone" is heart-rending, epitomized in the phrase "I yearn for the soothing bruise / of your embrace to ease the brittle / breaking of my heart…" The poem:

I wake from a dream of you
and know you are no longer
with me in the irredeemable

dark of the room we once
loved in, and I feel the moon
looming and the shudder of shadow
across the counterpane,
and I try to bring your face
once again into view,
smiling for me alone,
and I yearn for the soothing bruise
of your embrace to ease the brittle
breaking of my heart and the un-
renounceable ache
buried in the bone.

"Alight" is an expression of the lover´s desperation and yearning for his lost Anne. Both sad and reassuring, it tells us of Gutteridge's facility to involve the reader and pass on that desperate condition that ails him, that overwhelming wish to have Anne back:

I wake and find you alive
and loving beside me,
your eyes alight in the gloom,
and when I realize I'm still
in the demesne of dream (knowing
that the gods play us like pawns),
I want to hold you there,
safe and abiding, until
Doomsday dawns.

Gutteridge closes his book, *Lilacs in Lavender Light*, with "Bolt." Philosophical and nostalgic, he is able to interpret in the end the unstoppable cycles of time. His last poetic statement in the book (the two end lines) is axiomatic; it stays with us as all things true and high do. The poem:

They say that lightning never
strikes the same tree
twice, but in the summer
when I was almost me,
both of the maples that hugged
grandfather's house
and shaded my boyhood
games were struck down
by a single savage bolt,
and the home where I was lavished
by love and jolted with joy
and which I spun into a
dozen pulsing poems

and ringing rhymes, stood
there shivering in the sunshine
like a prude nude, and I knew
then that nothing is ever
the same again.

The Derelict Heart

The multi-published author comes again in 2020 thanks to Hidden Brook Press with another poetry book, *The Derelict Heart.* In an ode to family and love, Gutteridge continues to address those themes and sources that have given him a rich literary career and a way to word out the avalanche of feelings, experiences and memories knocking on this poet´s door, urging him to *write*, *write*, *write*, as Canadian poet Di Nardo has put it.

Allow me to quote the following fragment from E. K. Brown´s *On Canadian Poetry (ibidem, Brown)*: "One of our most gifted Canadian poet, novelists, Mr. Philip Albert Child, once remarked to me that a writer must be the obsequious servant of his demon, must rush to write when the demon stirs…" While the quotation goes on, points of coincidence can be detected in this excerpt in regard to Gutteridge´s life and poetic inclinations.

His start and development as a poet does enjoy personal but also contextual reinforcements, which channeled his budding talents making him "rush to write" when his personal demons stirred. In one of his poems, Gutteridge confesses "The unstoppable urge to write" ("Urge"), so similar to Canadian poet Glen Sorestad´s declaration, "I like the state I´m in when a poem takes hold and won´t let go" ("Six Reasons I Write Poems").

The Derelict Heart lists titles I have seen in other poetry books by Don, such as "Tropes," "Green and Growing," "Bolt," "Alight," "In the Bone," etc. As well, new titles show us Gutteridge´s broad repertoire and richness of style and wording to display many more pieces.

The Silence Between the Stars
In the gloaming over the River
flats (where we sometimes
flew our kites in the big-
breathed wind from the lake),
we played squat-tag
or May I? while the moon
loomed above our random
roaming and threw its mottled
light our way, while we waited
for the sky to darken and ignite
the silence between the stars.

"The Silence Between the Stars" opens *The Derelict Heart.* The seasoned reader will be gently affected by the "cosmic" atmosphere achieved by Gutteridge. Nostalgia and recollections of things done, sensations felt, decorate the poem. In all its "cosmicity" and beauty, the poem, though, succeeds in bringing together natural scenery and human emotion, in describing how the characters brought to the "the gloaming over the River / flats" and to where "the moon… / … threw its mottled / light" are charmed by the wonder of the moment (and the memories evoked), brilliantly painted in the finish lines "while we waited / for the sky to darken and ignite / the silence between the stars."

The personal and contextual reinforcements leading Don to write, which I referred to above, are more than palpable in the piece "Coming Home Lonely." We take delight in his creative use of language, personification greets us in the line "a parched / page avid for ink." The poem:

Coming home lonely
to a house that echoes when I wake it,
my mother migrained in her room,
father gone as usual,
brother seeking solace
further down the road
and, undisturbed, I batten
on a book, let my fancy
free, find a parched
page avid for ink,
and pen my first poem.

Gutteridge´s discoveries and explorations of love and the awakening of sex are rightly worded in many of his pieces. "Solo," "Gleam" and "Elapse" are some of the finest examples. The first one, "Solo," refers to the early infatuation stages of a boy amazed at the budding splendor of the female figure:

I saw her there but once
and that was more than enough:
Marybelle Cooper
curled on the sun-strummed
sands of Canatara
in her one-piece suit,
clinging to her girlish curves
like a lover's ruffling hands,
and I spent the rest of my day
humming without pause
like Orpheus on his lute, and singing
solo to Cupid's apt
applause.

The second one, "Gleam," less shy, more elaborate in its biblical-mythical allusions – and definitely more mischievous in its rhetorical question at the end – engages us for its sudden sentence breaks at the end of the lines, and its logical evolution from the previous one.

> *When Jo- dropped her panties*
> *and exposed the prize between*
> *her thighs, she had a gleam*
> *in her eye like Delilah's snipping*
> *Samson's lofty locks,*
> *like Salome's doing her death-*
> *dance unfrocked,*
> *like Bathsheba's dithering David,*
> *or like Eve's outwitting Adam*
> *with an ample apple, and what*
> *I want to know is did they*
> *enjoy the triumph of their titillation?*

Finally, "Elapse" fuses, in my modest understanding, the "initiation" spirit of "Solo" with the more direct "deployments" of "Gleam," still drawing a distinct, deferential line where sex and love meet and can be expressed naturally, gratifyingly. In addition, Gutteridge not only experiences and shares with us, he also helps us remember/assess our own ways of running into these once-in-a-lifetime events.

> *Marybelle Cooper,*
> *my best friend's cousin,*
> *stood behind the white*
> *picket fence that hugged*
> *our yard in her Tartan sweater*
> *under which her just—*
> *about breasts breathed*
> *serenely, and when she smiled*
> *my way, all the sonnets*
> *I longed to sing lapsed*
> *on my lips and when she smiled*
> *again, something tugged me*
> *aside and I knew for the first*
> *time what love was.*

The following lines are from Don´s poem "Itch": O it's hard not to be / immortal, for when we are gone, / we live on in the memories / of those who loved us alive..." When I read them, I recalled a poem I wrote to two friends of mine, "Cycles of Life." I hope readers will forgive me for quoting from my own poem: "When our parents go... / a part inside us follows them… // while the other part necessarily heads towards / tomorrow holding on to our beloved ones, those who / across the endless cycles of life / will safeguard too their memories of us."

"Itch" is a highly meditative, honest piece. Gutteridge treads on delicate, solemn themes with sobriety and grace, as he always does. Gutteridge´s poems have "… a sense of calming serenity." *(Shrabastee Chakraborty in a Hidden Brook Press release)* Death has been a luring mystery, one some people fear, some others respect, dismiss as unimportant – even rush valiantly towards, and others just embrace as the irreversible end side of life. I think Gutteridge rises to the occasion provided by the subject and approaches it with poise. True to his penmanship, Don opens the poem with a useful expressive means, litotes (or meiosis): "…it's hard not to be / immortal."

It is defined as an "understatement in which an affirmative is expressed by the negative of the contrary (as in "not a bad singer" or "not unhappy")" *(Taken from Merriam-Webster Collegiate® Dictionary).* It is a "kind of double negative… when two negative words form a positive statement." *(Taken from a VOA radio broadcast. Adam Brock as writer and producer for VOA Learning English, and Ashley Thompson as editor)* Gutteridge resourcefully uses its stylistic potential in his poem:

O it's hard not to be
immortal, for when we are gone,
we live on in the memories
of those who loved us alive
and in the stories they tell
of us when day draws down
and we become part of the lore
that thrives wherever there are
humans with an itch for history,
and so it is, I look upon
my demise with no regard
for endings, compromise
or polite applause, certain
that, against the odds,
the long sentence, my life,
will not be periodic.

Gutteridge´s pondering on poetry making reaches a mature degree in "Bard." The word *bard* quickly sparks the notion of poets from medieval times, is mostly used in special literary registers, and refers also to minstrels, musicians, singers, troubadours, holding a historic, esoteric hue (it is remarkable how the poet adds the adjective *arcane* to the "business / of being a bard" as he closes the piece). Gutteridge aims at that: the stylistic value of the word serves the poet´s purpose well. The poem also speaks of his total surrendering to poetry, how it has charted his life´s course and made it significant, complete; how it allowed him to put in words his condition of being "born / to pain and poetry." The poem is a hymn to the craft of poetry writing, to its undeniable allure:

I find it hard to imagine
a life without the wizardry
of words: the nuances of nouns
and verbs surging: pinned
in the prism of a poem, where rhyme
has its reasons and rhythm is what
the heart hears in the silence
between beats and simile
has its seasons, and I was born
to pain and poetry, and longed
to embrace the arcane business
of being a bard.

But Gutteridge does not solely write poems to family, friends, memories, poetry. He is also an observant, committed and sentient writer, who is impacted by social events and misfortunes. His poem "I Can´t Breathe" is eloquent prove of that. Don, having been deeply hurt by the awful events that led to the tragic murder of George Floyd, dedicated this heartfelt piece to him.

In the form of dialogue, Gutteridge talks to Floyd, immortalizing (Gutteridge and thousands of people around the world brandish it now as an accusatory phrase against the killers) Floyd´s agonizing cry "I Can´t Breathe" while life was brutally crushed out of him.

While the world watched, a man
with a heart harried by hatred,
knelt upon your neck
in a parody of prayer, deaf
to your plea: "I can't breathe!",
a phrase unfurled like a beacon
of outrage and carried
to far continents, wherever
men and women looked
to love to turn the page
on racial violence, and some-
where, miles from the nearest
bigot, you: looking down
and forgiving, your eyes wreathed
in smiles.

In another poem, we return to the poet´s most striking themes, his beloved Anne and Tom. See how he starts "Hymn":

I've spent more than a life-
time inking the world
with poems and stories, and you
have so enthused my Muse
that words flow to the
pristine page…

See how he explains his losses and his sad muses:

… when you left me bereft,
I limned a lyric alive,
a dolorous hymn to what
has been lost…

And finally see how he – as he has done so many times – rises above pain, finds succor in love and ends the poem:

… but love
is more diligent than Death
and we all survived.

In his poem "Dialogue," Gutteridge clearly exposes the relationship between his poems and his entire life. Quintessentially metaphorical, he pairs the "dialogue between / me and myself…// I wax / iambic…" and is "happy to be / in this long conversation…" which he sums up as "my life":

My poems are a dialogue between
me and myself, and I sing
sonnets to civility, ballads
to my beloved, some gist
caught up in a couplet,
quatrains rife with rhyme,
and when I speak, I wax
iambic, happy to be
in this long conversation,
my life.

"I wake from a dream of you" is an undoubtedly suggestive line used by Don in many other poems to talk about his recurring oniric encounters with his Anne (post-dream realization she is not with him, or the poet´s fantasies she *is still* there), an emotive relief valve to the grief in his mind. He has also come up with variations from this matrix (I exemplified that elsewhere before. More examples are found in *The Derelict Heart*: "The Far Side of the Dark," "Possible," "Pristine," "Distance," etc.), as is the case of our next poem, "When the Dream Ends."

In it, Don begins with "I wake and feel the bend / of your body, but when the dream / ends…" However heartrending his loss is, and how moving his depiction of loss is, the poet stunningly manages to find hope, courage, balance in stirring lines that combine the exquisite relish of love felt by the poet and his expert utilization of expressive means, such as the sublime simile "like the incoming rush / of combers on a star-lit lake…":

> *… I thank the all-seeing*
> *gods for the tender years*
> *our love thrived and grew*
> *like the incoming rush*
> *of combers on a star-lit*
> *lake…*

Let´s have the whole poem, a magnificent example of creative writing devoted to love especially, admirably summarized by Gutteridge in the last two lines:

> *I wake and feel the bend*
> *of your body, but when the dream*
> *ends, I am alone in the*
> *condoning dark and you*
> *are still unalive,*
> *but I thank the all-seeing*
> *gods for the tender years*
> *our love thrived and grew*
> *like the incoming rush*
> *of combers on a star-lit*
> *lake and, like larks in the amber*
> *air, we sang the same*
> *home-grown song*
> *and travelled true to the spirit*
> *that bound us beautiful,*
> *and even in death you are*
> *the breath of my being.*

I close my comments on *The Derelict Heart* with the poem from which a line entitles the book and continues the passionate, overwhelming thematic course set in our previous piece. "Where No Light Goes" keeps us riveted to Don´s writing. With the book and the poem, we must breathe in and out at times. His undeterred allegiance to the love of his life strikes a light of veneration in us. Let´s end our journey across this book with it:

You managed to dodge Death
for eighty-three years,
and for five decades of those
we were never apart, your breath
as predictable as the sun licking
a rose with light or a breeze
bullying leaves or a peregrine
hefting Heaven, and now
that you are gone where no
light goes, I'll strive
to remember you: alive and fully
free, your love forever
lodged in my derelict heart.

The anthology, Hearthbeat

Gutteridge is an accomplished writer and poet but he has also edited poetry anthologies. In 2020, Hidden Brook Press published his warm *Hearthbeat.* Fifty-nine poets, including the book´s editor, capture in heart-warming wording and fine style the sometimes time-diluted – or apparently passé-in-these-modern-hectic-days – idea of what family really means.

I have been motivated by the fortunate realization that Canadian poets do have an "umbilical" connection with their roots, understood as a national and family historic construction of an individual identity. It tells them where they come from and defines them, lighting up their paths: the hearth, aptly registered by Webster´s dictionary, digital version, as "home and family life: the joys of hearth and home." Gutteridge is the mastermind that reveals it for us.

Don Gutteridge, one of the few authors who appear in my three books on Canadian poetry, understandably left his own poetry for the end. Don opened his book with a statement, "To the core called family." There is no better introduction to a collection of poetry that celebrates the institution of family in its varied manifestations and ramifications. When we read Don´s "Going," our hearts leap out to the grieving soul that writes these beautifully sad lines. However, we seek to find necessary, unavoidable comfort in the closing line…

"When I first saw you
in that incubator
taking baby breaths,
your wee fingers still
wizened from the womb, glancing
off any horizon,

I didn't think we'd see you
growing golden into your bones,
but we did, and you grew anew
each loving day
you gave us, and when Death
drew you into its darkness,
we mourned your lonely going,
knowing you would never be old."

As a compilation, one of the editor´s virtues is in the group of poets summoned to make this book come true. Such choice granted from the beginning the literary-sentimental value of what we have in our hands today.

I quote from a poem by Don, "The Way Home": "The way home is thru / the heart, every blood-beat / hums with remembrance."

I stated in my review book that "Gutteridge´s *Point Taken* has brought happiness and homesickness to my mind." So has this new Hidden Brook Press publication. *Hearthbeat* honors these quotations from cover to cover: family ties and memories beat in the mists of time never to fade because there are poets, editors and publishers who safeguard and remind us, readers, of the worth of family roots.

Where it comes to remembering life and living, love and loving; we will always have Gutteridge shining on both sides of life´s tunnel in this anthology and in his books: he is convinced that who leads us into, through and out of existence is family. Poetry certainly eases the passage and honors the family factor.

Into the Milkweed Meadow

As I have often stated, landscape and seasons bewilder and entice Canadian poets. It has been so since the emergence of Canadian poetry. Gutteridge´s book *Into the Milkweed Meadow* (Hidden Brook Press, 2021) is an example of this. It is more than that too. His opening poem, "A-Burst," shows an engaged poet, who observes in detail and amazement – even anticipates – the miracle of spring. The title prepares the reader for the moment but what comes is an explosion of life and movement.

Gutteridge foresees, describes, fills the lines with provocative words, *detonate, fling, full arousal, bruising, uncrumbling* and vivid phrases, "*rain-sated clods, / and lusting for air and a tease / of the come-summer breeze…*" to close elevating even more the seasonal ecstasy in his allusion to Eden and masterfully treating alliteration (repetition of "b" in the final words).

Let´s enjoy his piece fully, as fully as the way his gifted hand depicts what is coming:

On the just-cusp of Spring,
seedlings, breeding in the dark
under the earth, detonate,
flinging their shoots, in full

arousal, bruising upwards,
uncrumbling as they go,
rain-sated clods,
and lusting for air and a tease
of the come-summer breeze,
they sprout loudly in twos
and threes, and the world
turns as green as the groomed
demesnes of Eden – a-burst
with birthing and bloom.

The poet goes beyond odes to the seasons blending them in his next poem, "What is More," with his strong childhood memories, a theme I have previously commented on in his works. He invites us into the piece with "*Summer was the season strung / between June and September.*" As the poem advances, it takes us into a world of excellent epithets (*sun-thumbed streets*, *heat-seizing sands*, *blue-bellied lake*) to culminate in a hyperbolic – yet psychologically powerful – state of mind, "*for we were easy / in our bones and, what is more, / immortal.*": (excerpts)

Summer was the season strung
between June and September
when we were young enough
to be free and combed
the sun-thumbed streets
for stray empties loitering
in nooks and crannies, whose
two-penny return
would buy us a grab-bag
or a brace of gumballs,
and we lazed away amber
afternoons on Canatara's
heat-seizing sands
and dove for bottle-caps
in our blue-bellied lake
and compared shy erections
in the boys' change-room
with its spy-dy hole and took
no guff from anyone
elder than us, well-meaning
or goitered, for we were easy
in our bones and, what is more,
immortal.

Another remarkable poem is "True." Short, concise, pictorial in the account of colors that assist the reader in grasping the scene, it opens a reality the poet freezes, conveying a state of silent sadness. The widow seeks "*surcease of sorrow*," as Poe would say, in nature again, so Gutteridge grants the garden a healing sense, a lifesaver status.

Explaining the cause of the woman´s widowhood (loss in general terms, a condition the poet himself has suffered), the poet briefly mentions the bereaving cruelty of war, and magnifies the woman´s suffering with the "still-in-her-prime" remark. How he succeeds in relating the blooms with her memories proposes the notion of pain being somehow – or necessarily –soothed by new life, an idea that is validated in the last line: (a memory) "… *true and untarnished by Time*." She has idealized her "*having loved*."

The young woman must channel her loss, which has curtailed her otherwise promising life, tending a garden brimming with life. As a reader, I can go deeper into the surface of the poem: it presents the fact but also opens a diversity of possibilities of what could have happened – what *may* happen in the future of a woman "*still in her prime*" – in my mind. Below, the whole poem:

Missus Bray, widowed
by war and still in her prime,
let her grieving flow
through the flowers that
garnished her garden, and each
bloom: crimson, gold
or blue, brought to her mind
a memory of having loved,
true and untarnished by Time.

Memories, childhood, images deeply guarded in the poet´s mind, reminiscences rekindled, revisited and re-felt are nostalgically engraved in "Meme." Let´s notice the contemplative words that open the poem, where I appreciate the poet´s oxymoronic deed in "quiet-collusion":

My village lies in quiet
collusion with the sun, long
shadows lean lengthwise
from houses that held me hostage
for a dozen seasons…

Personification helps us understand Gutteridge´s sentimental connection with what surrounds him in the previous last two lines. I pick calm, almost relieved, gratefulness that comes from realizing things are about the same in his dear Point Edward: (excerpts)

streets
my feet read like a bard's
Braille, sit just as
they did when I roamed them //
and the Bridge still skewers
the sky and Mara's roof
still tilts as it did
when Jerry and I swam
our summers away in the Lake

However, within such idyllic settings, there are also gone parts, those time and tide and progress took away. Gutteridge hurts in these lines:

… and the school
where I scribbled the first
line of an interminable epic
is now gone under the wrecker's
ball, and I am as reluctant
to leave this meme of memory
as a bride her epithalamium
or a groom his darling's garland

Here, the whole poem:

Meme
Point Edward: July 2018

My village lies in quiet
collusion with the sun, long
shadows lean lengthwise
from houses that held me hostage
for a dozen seasons, and streets
my feet read like a bard's
Braille, sit just as
they did when I roamed them
like LaSalle on a sortie, combing
for news of a better world,
and the Bridge still skewers
the sky and Mara's roof
still tilts as it did
when Jerry and I swam
our summers away in the Lake
as big and as blue as the Baltic,

with dunes a-doze in the hectic
noontide light, and the school
where I scribbled the first
line of an interminable epic
is now gone under the wrecker's
ball, and I am as reluctant
to leave this meme of memory
as a bride her epithalamium
or a groom his darling's garland

Gutteridge re-explores his origins not only as a man but also, and consistently, as a poet. Our next poem talks about his inspirations and first poetic attempts (also addressed in "A Grammar for Grief" or "Consolation"):

Rose

And here I am walking
the beach at Canatara
with its silken, Saharan sands
and a sun hung above,
as yellow as a bruised moon
looking for a world to enlighten
and blooming anew in the wombed
blue of the Lake I was young
enough to dream into being,
and on a far horizon, herring-
gulls levitate in loops
and cliff-swallows swerve
serenely over the dunes
I once reconnoitred
like some lunatic LaSalle,
and here is where I found
the words to ignite the poem
that grew inside me like a rose
exploding in the bone.

It is outstanding how the poet starts the poem with "*And...*" planting in the reader the legitimate sensation of the many things *before* this moment. I can think of a poet who is dreaming, or is actually walking the beach, imbued with an environment that fills him both physically and emotionally. The poem is highly metaphorical. Imagery flows as he rests his gaze upon each element he then proceeds to describe out of an innermost motivation: (excerpts)

the beach at Canatara
with its silken, Saharan sands… //
… bruised moon
looking for a world to enlighten
and blooming anew in the wombed
blue of the Lake…

As a closer, a simile, "*the poem / that grew inside me like a rose.*" Semantically attached to the notion of delicacy, the rose (the poem! – it evoked in me Umberto Eco´s 1980 novel *The Name of the Rose*), nonetheless, comes to life in an explosion that emerges from the poet´s bone. That is how he sees his initiation as one: we are brought to the revelation that he is a context-born writer. A truly inspirational milieu forged him: "*and here is where I found / the words to ignite the poem.*"

Airs of polysyndeton auspiciously blow with "*and*" (six in the poem). This stylistic device is usually combined with enumeration to achieve rhythm. Enumeration, being "frequently used to depict scenery," *(Taken from Stylistics, Galperin I. R., 1981)* is used in the poem to depict realities that make the poet´s heart grow fonder, while polysyndeton integrates "elements of thought into one whole" *(ibidem)* in a succession of things that acquire self-standing significance. Each aspect caught by the poet´s eye has a unique relevance, so laid out by him.

If we had Gutteridge sharing his origins in the previous poem, in "A-Buzz" we enter his well-conceived, naturally candid and eloquent awakening to love/sex. Simple, bordering on a casual kid´s story-telling, the piece recreates that sudden discovery of love through a character we have often seen in his oeuvre, Nancy Mara. The end lines are quite intense, as a perfect "companion" for the title and suitable coda to what the poet intends to narrate and make the reader be ready for. Below, the whole poem:

Nancy Mara, in her one-
piece suit, lies
belly-down on Canatara's
beach in its sun-seethed
sand, and for a stunned second
my breathing stalls, and my heart
purrs at the sight of wind-
thumbed thighs, and all
the boys are a-buzz, wondering
if this is what beauty was,
and something asleep
inside me leaps towards
light.

Other salient poems in the book refer to the love/sex aspect of Gutteridge´s life. One of them is "Clinch" (You can also read "Translation," "Demure" or a variation piece, "Blister," etc.). Somewhat jocose, it introduces the inevitable love sting mingled with the sex component, neatly described by the poet. Aptly-chosen expressive means propel the poem along its lines, "… *she bloomed like a slow rose / in a lash of light…*" (a simile), "… *my tongue / hummed and hawed…*" (onomatopoeic instances), and a superb hyperbolic end, "*I knew even then / that somewhere the Earth / had moved an inch on its axis.*" Let´s have the poem in full:

Shirley was the first girl
no longer to be just
a pal, and I watched in awe
as she bloomed like a slow rose
in a lash of light, and when
she smiled my way, my tongue
hummed and hawed as I tried
not to ogle the fresh bevels
of her body or day-dream
a libidinous clinch,
for I knew even then
that somewhere the Earth
had moved an inch on its axis.

As he has done in his other poetry books, Gutteridge does not forget his friends. A poem sprinkled with sincere friendship and literary allusions, "Friend" leaves a sweet taste in me. I studied Mark Twain in college yet had devoured Tom Sawyer more than once in my teenage years, later urged my daughter to read it too, so I clicked with the poem in more than one way. Intimacy is achieved as the poem was conceived as a dialogue between the poet and his friend. It adds to the emotions sparked and the memories ignited. Let´s have it:

O how I envied you,
riding your lovingly-crafted
raft like a hero in a
Mark Twain novel,
down the Mississippi
where our fantasies ended,
and me, unable to swim,
forlorn on the riverbank,
wishing I had the pluck
to play Tom to your Huck,
but you just grinned at me
as you paddled away, and said
"I'm still your friend"

The beauty of love comes in impeccable form with "Muted." See how he ends the poem, an excitingly sculpted finish: "*... and when at last / our bodies greet in full- / blooded ease, vistas / unroll, and in that cleaved / seizing, our souls are broken / and made whole again.*" Read the whole piece:

We whisper words of love
as if this feeling is too
fragile to be spoken above
a decibel, but still they are heard
as sweet as sunlight silking
the sill below the window
that lets the world in
to wonder at our muted
passion, and when at last
our bodies greet in full-
blooded ease, vistas
unroll, and in that cleaved
seizing, our souls are broken
and made whole again.

The man, the romantic, the endless lover, Gutteridge overwhelms me once more with "Doon." The poem has references to epic, legendary events, the search for the Holy Grail, and characters, Galahad, that heighten its mood, but its message transcends those. Sentimental, gentle, imagery-rich, the poem is a dialogue, in retrospective, with his beloved Anne.

It is abundant in alliteration as well: "When we went walking the woods," "I let / the light limning your eyes / linger in mine...," "the deep December dark," "simmered, softened and lapsed," a device that "aims at imparting a melodic effect to the utterance" and provides an "emotional atmosphere which each reader interprets for himself." *(ibidem, Galperin)* Below, the poem:

When we went walking the woods
below Doon under a sky
stitched with stars and a moon
above us, groomed luminous,
I held your hand like Galahad
cupping the Grail or a pilgrim
prizing a shrine, and I let
the light limning your eyes
linger in mine and brim
the deep December dark,
and this was a night we'll remember
long after that first

voluptuous surge of affection
has simmered, softened and lapsed
into love.

Nevertheless, the cusp, to me, of the profoundly sensitive, enamored poet comes with "Lustrous." Here Gutteridge displays his full-fledged lyricism from start to end. In my readings of contemporary Canadian greats I have come across decidedly sentient pieces, like John B. Lee´s "One Leaf in the Breath of the World" or "I Wake to Breathe Your Beauty In." Gutteridge has equally made me sigh with his poem (Gutteridge includes a poem to Lee in the book, "A-Bloom").

Sweetness, melancholy, devotion, cherishing and commitment shine in the poem. Gutteridge rises from his oneiric realm, "*I wake from a dream of you, / and you are with me once more…*" where he is beside his Anne – and continues to be after he wakes! The poem then walks us across his favorite mementoes and closes with a pledge of unending love, passionate, faithful. Below, the piece:

I wake from a dream of you,
and you are with me once more,
alive in all your loveliness,
and we are ambling the pristine
pastures of Gibbons as we did*
when our love was young and honeyed
with hope, a daylight moon
above us like a silvered bloom,
a breeze buffeting your hair
agleam, and our hands enlinked
as if touch were tenderness
enough – and I want to drown
in the lustrous lake of your eyes
and love you unbibbed
until the world dooms or dies.

My comments should close with the poem Gutteridge took a line from ("*Into the milkweed meadow*") to entitle the whole book, "Finding Felicity." Sublime and reflective in its essence, attached to nature, one classic leitmotif in Canadian writers, the poem makes the reader walk as the poet walks; it makes the reader feel the way the poet feels, and finally, it heads towards that recurring, unavoidable core theme in Gutteridge, his Anne.
The last lines suggest more than the poet probably expected, or imagined, when he wrote it. They utterly stand as the best guide in this life: "*find / felicity, and be.*" The poem:

Into the milkweed meadow
once more, breaking
open as we go the pouched

pods and watching their silkening
insides eddy the air,
here where grasshoppers
fling from the fringes like sassy
acrobats, and adders with bloated
throats puff umbrage,
and larks decorate the day
with song and marsh marigolds
mellow with infusions from the
celebrating sun
and cattails tuft in a buffeting
breeze: and I dream you here
with me, night upon night,
and bring you back alive
to meander meadows, find
felicity, and be.

In 2021 Hidden Brook Press also published Gutteridge´s *More Boding than Blood.* With its opening poem, which entitles the book, we are welcome once more to the idyllic remembrances of *Into the Milkweed Meadow*, colored with metaphorical phrases,

If you had lived but one
more day, I would have walked you
into the milkweed meadow
where butterflies unbutton
their wings…

Dialogic, as many of Gutteridge´s pieces, the poem breathes with a touching aura. Towards the end, references to how the poet´s poetry came to be, how it found inspiration is confessed:

… "So this is where the poems
gave birth to themselves?"
and I would reply, "Here
and in the kind of love
you brought me, more boding
than blood, more basic
than bone."

Below, the poem in full:
If you had lived but one
more day, I would have walked you
into the milkweed meadow

where butterflies unbutton
their wings to bask on the breeze
and puckered pods, lanced
by light, expose their silken
sofas and larks sweeten
the air with saccharine song
and grasshoppers fling
free of gravity on tiny
trapezes and puff-adders
sputter loud enough
to frighten the frogs holidaying
on the pond and bulrushes
fluff their rusted coiffures –
and you would have said,
"So this is where the poems
gave birth to themselves?"
and I would reply, "Here
and in the kind of love
you brought me, more boding
than blood, more basic
than bone."

On the same reminiscing chord, but now more meditative and attempting to find readjustment – or some sort of explanation – to the losses he suffers, the poet writes "Beyond Hope,"

If there were a god dispensing
kudos and brickbats,
I could curse him for letting Tom die,
but I am not a man
of belief in matters beyond
hope, and so my grief
must bleed leeward to brood
in the bone, and my cries for relief
find no home,
here or in Heaven.

The poem pierces into our own experiences in more than one sting of its grief. The line "and my cries for relief / find no home" instantly brought to me Shakespeare´s Sonnet XXIX (excerpt), "And trouble deaf heaven with my bootless cries, / And look upon myself, and curse my fate… // … For thy sweet love remembered such wealth brings / That then I scorn to change my state with kings." Readers of Shakespeare and Gutteridge will immediately realize that despite their perfectly human complaints, in the end they both find consolation in their "sweet love remembered".

Missus Bray, a familiar character in many of his poems, comes again in "Festooned," a gentle poem where the poet places the widow in a between-dreams state, one that pushes her across her bereft condition. The poem:

Missus Bray dreamed
of blooms in her garden,
festooned with flowers of every
ilk, and when the sun
came up, it soothed
the day's bouquets as soft
as any satin or silk,
and she bid them bask in the
purview of her praise,
and when night came down,
she dreamed again of daisies
and daffodils in their delight
and let her widowed heart
teem.

A particularly interesting poem is "Rhyme," where the poet "theorizes" about his poetic background and his relation with poetry. Besides describing his initial urges, contemplating his inspirational milieus and analyzing how it all might have started in his life, Gutteridge acknowledges the lure of a poem, the breeding ground that was his village poetically speaking, without relinquishing the essences he has been so faithful to, rhythm, rhyme, expressive means. The poem:

My poems come from somewhere
deep within the bardic
bone, where the id dozes
in ribald repose, until
the itch to beget grips it
bidden, and words flow
into the easy iambic of an ode
or the supple couplets of a balladeer's
banter, and I've spent the better
part of a lifetime pillaging
the voluminous root of the home-
ground and the village that hatched me
whole into a world rich
with ritual and rhyme.

Many have been the classic influences on Don´s work. One of them is Emily Dickinson. In a poem that pays tribute to her both in structure, syntactic-semantic compactness and message, we enjoy his thoughts and homage comments on one of the most revered poetesses of all time. Gutteridge introduces capitalized words from Dickinson´s own poems (Death, Mortality), confesses to be angry at God at the start but later understands the power of "each forgiving season" and the fact, as he tells us in other poems, that "love / lives on." The poem:

Where Love Lives
With a nod to Emily D
When God took your breath
away and let your body
be, I cursed Him and a universe
where Death and his dam, Mortality,
gamble our chances agley,
but with the coming of each
forgiving dawn, love
lives on.

"I wake from a dream of you" (line used in other poems as well, "In the Bone" (from *Lilacs in Lavender Light*); "Lustrous" (from *Into the Milkweed Meadow*); "Radiant" (in this book); "Unexempt" in a slight variation, "I wake from a troubled sleep / having dreamt you are still alive," (from *Invincible Ink*), appears now in our next poem, "Serendipity," one of the numberless pieces Gutteridge has written to his Anne.

The poet reminisces, ponders on desires and longings he would have wanted to eternalize, and once more – as in the previous poem, "Where Love Lives" – he finds shelter and consolation in "we beat / the odds for fifty-seven years / of loving and the lyric of laughter." He remains loyal to his style: alliterative units providing the rhythm Gutteridge so much appreciates in writing poetry ("teeming of its touch," "serendipity of soul," "fretful fury" and "loving and the lyric of laughter").
The poem:

I wake from a dream of you
in my arms once again,
letting our bodies be,
as they were when our love was young
and each moon-soothed
evening thereafter we renewed
the teeming of its touch
and its serendipity of soul,
and I wanted so much
to keep you free from all
harm, from the fretful fury
of a world where the gods demur
and deny, and a love like ours

would falter and die, but we beat
the odds for fifty-seven years
of loving and the lyric of laughter.

I chose "Lexicon" as the poem to finish my comments on *More Boding than Blood.* Being poetry and life two central motifs in Don´s writing, this poem honors them inasmuch as it honors the poetic urges the burning inside a poet and need to find expression. Written with passion and a maturity that we know accompanies Gutteridge, it harmonizes nostalgia, fortitude, tenderness, attitude.
The poet knows where his writing comes from, "My poems arise like geysers / from some burrow abiding / in the bone or, when the Muse / is muted, like a slow budding / in the blood..." He knows who the most important source is, "gushing or aglow / they are rooted in the kind of love / you brought to me from the / morning you were born..." and, as the great poet he is, he is well aware poetry is molded in the converging blend of the outside ("looted from the lexicon") and the inside ("seasoned in my genes"). Whatever inspirations vibrate in the poet, his ultimate motivations are to be indisputably found in love, his most recurring theme. Let´s have this poem:

My poems arise like geysers
from some burrow abiding
in the bone or, when the Muse
is muted, like a slow budding
in the blood, but gushing or aglow
they are rooted in the kind of love
you brought to me from the
morning you were born and sought
my adoring eyes and all
the days of our doting dalliance,
until you sallied astray,
and so it is I pen
these lines, looted from the lexicon
and seasoned in my genes, to say
again how much you've sanctified
my life.

With his partially exploratory inquiry into and recompilation of earlier works, Don Gutteridge marches solidly along 2021 also publishing *Where Rivers Run Deep* with Hidden Brook Press. The book is a compendium of his narratives from 1962 to 1972, which include: Part One of *Death at Quebec and Other Poems* (Fiddlehead Books, 1971), *Saying Grace: An Elegy* (Fiddlehead Books, 1972).

In my analyses of his early books I quoted isolated, yet representative, excerpts of his poems. I stated at the beginning of this book that readers would relish in the spirituality of Don's words and the deep-seated recognition of the earth's significance, acknowledging it as an animate being. *Where Rivers Run Deep* is not just a title. It embodies the profundity that enriches the human soul and lifts it up to a higher level of cognizance and edification on what surrounds the human being. That *Where* is not *any*where; it is the origin, the foundation, the becoming aware. Let´s read "Riel 1":

I am a man
as any man:
hands to know
the plough's hand
deeper in the earth,
hair to feel
the wind's
passing thru
and grasses move,
eyes to let
the sky's
vastness in
to deeper skies
I only know
because
my hands
my hair
these eyes
become a voice
to say
I am a man

The poem exudes a self-recognition of man, his deep bond with nature and the construal of a link that has always been there, and granted man "… a voice / to say / I am a man" Resounding words, yet simple and direct, ring in our ears. Readers will agree that the poem´s structure does respond to the very essence of its nature and the nature of the man´s declaration: direct, proud, short, enumerative lines, as strong as the thought being voiced by the poet.

Another examination of the mind and the soul is "5 The Last Word":

Do our voices
reach out
from the past
escape the text
of history book
or turn
of politician's tongue,
describe a

true syllable
of what we knew
and still know
though words
are water
one can feel
and not define?

Or could there be
some secret part
of north
some centre
we never touched
in all our wandering,
some syllable
of silence
our tongues
did not dare
to desecrate,
some holy core
whose seed
we could not hope
to recognize as
altars running
fountains thru
the deep
earth-colour
of our blood

The poem is also critical, open and sincere in questioning social events or characters, the intricacies of the mind and the search for answers that seem to evade the poet as he carves with strength and determination the thoughts poured into this piece.

The Section *Saying Grace: An Elegy* posed a challenge to me (I lost my mother so unexpectedly). Gutteridge led me through the corridors of being born:

1
At my birth
we shared the
same pain
your blood
rubbed my eyes
open to light
heaved in

the dark
rushed out with my
my cry as your
scream squeezed
the lights shut
* * *
When I burst
headlong into this
world my
lungs exploded
just as your
appendix burst
like a time-bomb
ticking in its
womb
only one of us
made it whole

Also of growing and experiencing, (excerpt)

but mostly it was love
leading us both and together
down to the lake's edge,
to look out and over and
never see the other side,
feeling (as one) the waves
tremble at our feet

And his mother´s death,

2
That day
when I touched your dead hand
my skin quickened,
out of habit I whispered
in your ear not wanting
to wake you too sudden,
but you lay there
aloof
dissembling sleep
insisting even when I
shook your wrist
like a stick (refusing breath:

no man / husband / son
would waken you that day)
after a while
it occurred to me
you were not there:
the casket of your flesh
confirmed it.

In all of the poems, the same balance of style, the inner poetic voice rendering lyrical, composed lines, which differ, structurally speaking (this section and the previous one), from most of the Gutteridge books I studied before. The ideas flow differently, in fragments of meditation that is sometimes apparently erratic, then coherently conceived in the speaker´s mind and concretized in his manner of reflecting it.

The pieces that follow in the book read like trains of quizzical/curious considerations, which the poet skillfully raises to the rank in many cases of epigrams, even proverbs. There are statements about a variety of subjects, all of them in close interconnectedness with the poet´s personal life and social concerns; all of them showing a cultivated writer, who knows how to sprinkle irony, humor, concepts, private glimpses, cultural/literary allusions, locations, occurrences, etc.: it is the maelstrom of thoughts passing through the poet´s mental sieve. And he dares to disclose them all and share them.

In my humble view, Gutteridge´s oeuvre ought to be approached whole, as a long narrative, didactic chronicle, and a thick but original treatise that affords to have gentility of composition, love and fortitude commingling with a more than necessarily serious, well-knitted, impressive testimony of a lifetime.

I finish my analyses of Gutteridge´s work with the penultimate piece in the book, "6." Somehow it summarizes Gutteridge´s position and dedication to writing, prompted by his life, the life of others, the world around him (close or far) and the never-ending mystery of the muses:

Pain writes poems
on a human face,
crooked lines,
scrawled flesh.
We make poems
with our skin / our bones,
words obey
dance the tune
of our pain

How many lines
must I scrawl

from the mask
of your runed face?
And what grace
in obedient words,
transfigured pain?
What gain
when we both die
in the rending syllable
of the last poem?

Ploughing the Home Ground
Ploughing Deep with Don Gutteridge: Scholarship and Heart

The book *Ploughing the Home Ground* by Don Gutteridge, wisely published by QuodSermo Publishing, 2021, is a compendium of some of Don Gutteridge´s vibrant, certainly scholarly essays even though Gutteridge contests, in his modesty, that neither him nor his writings are scholarly but the scholar is there, deep within the learned man and felt-to-the-poet´s-core in his views on Canadian literature. Don Gutteridge shows his broad tessitura as a writer: poetry is his love but prose and essay writing have comfortable room in his heart.

Gutteridge ploughs deep and turns the soil of his sacred lit-land, as he eloquently expresses in his opening essay, "I am hopelessly a Canadian, having been born, raised, educated, and professionally turned out in an area not more than sixty miles in diameter, whose centre happens to be London, Ontario."

In a language that is elaborate yet direct, argumentative yet straightforward to the point, we walk through his early works that raise interesting questions – and definitely provide valid answers – related to issues regarding not just literature and poetics but also historical and social concerns. Don cannot, nor does he want to, constrain the poet in him. His poetic spirit and his wittiness throb in every piece. Gutteridge theorizes, willingly or not, engaged in a passionate elucidation and unraveling of burning aspects, which have intrigued, affected and defined his beloved nation and more specific lit contexts and production.

In terms of the poet´s endeavor to point the exploring finger at lit-related many-sided angles and realities that even extend their webs into our present day, notice, for example, his explanation on the idea of myth, stated in his second essay: "The second point to be made here is that the arts, and literature in particular, have traditionally been the repository for myths, the myths of the individual writer fashioning his work of art and through it the myths of the society out of which and for whom he is writing." His reflections on the subject are eye openers in more than one sense, and throw light – personally insightful – on a carefully mapped out route he charts for us.

Moving from the general topics I have mentioned above, Gutteridge also brings to the readers his analyses on top writers, like Margaret Atwood – or pays tribute to artists, the Group of Seven – and their works. He dissects and evidences, however unpretentious he reminds us his studies to be, the fibers, intents, meaning and value of their oeuvre, not to mention their transcendent character.

I was particularly attracted to his essay "The Coherence of Consonance in Poetry." A devoted admirer of British, American and Canadian poets, and as a professor of English Stylistics at the University of Holguin, I always enjoyed – and attempted to write my early poems using them – the rich variety of expressive means in language, especially phonetic ones.

In his essay, Gutteridge takes us by the hand and discloses the power and appeal of such resources, proving once more his erudition on the subject and his command in practice (his poems are masterpieces). See how he begins his essay: "There has been a great deal of critical writing about sound values, metre and rhythm in poetry. It is often a very erudite and rarefied excursion. One may reasonably ask what is left to be said on the subject." Nevertheless, he does offer a significant contribution to the matter, reflected in both his fervent renderings and his depth of perspective.

My reading priorities as a Stylistics professor in the English Major at Holguin University have an asset in his paper, inasmuch as he disserts on the topic and exemplifies with one of those classics I love, Emily Dickinson.

The book closes with an Appendix that presents two valuable essays on Gutteridge´s own work. In short, Gutteridge´s knowledge of and contribution to the lit mosaic are vast, impressive and necessary. It suffices to take our hats off but then we see the man whose gifted mind emulates with his poet´s heart.

While preparing my book *Five Canadian poets: Analytical essays on James Deahl, John B. Lee, Don Gutteridge, Glen Sorestad, A.F. Moritz* (QuodSermo Publishing, 2021), I asked him (and the other four poets), "Could you just irreversibly stop writing poetry?" His reply was: "Nothing short of a stroke could stop me from writing poetry… I seem to dream poems and wake up writing them... I am very fortunate that the Muse has never let me down."

Awesome.

QuodSermo Publishing does well in honoring one of Canada´s finest men of letters, poets and human beings, and in doing so it adds prestige to its quintessential role of promoting the best of Canadian literature, culture – and soul.

Conclusion

Don Gutteridge has his singular style, comfortably placed within a latent universality. He is recipient, repository and paradigm at the same time. He is committed to his land, evidenced when we read his poems and notice references to nature, to geographies and seasons, to vast maps of wildlife and wilderness.

In Gutteridge, there is the unavoidable, deeply-ingrained family-friend-wife leitmotif. About his family poems, Emily-Jane Hills Orford said, "Special family connections. The simplicity of treasured family moments…" *(Hidden Brook Press release)* She added, "I have read a number of Don Gutteridge's poems over the years and I continue to marvel at his ability to capture the simplest of moments in a capsule and make it grander than life with his poetic observations." *(ibidem)*

I have often stated that "Canadian poets exceed in wording, honoring and recalling facts, events, people, and names." Don´s poems invariably state whom they were written for. Particularly moving are the ones written to Anne, his wife, and to Tom, his grandson.

Even though sadness is present in the cry of the bereaved man, Don finds consolation in beauty and memories. The poet does not complain or lament forever: he sees a form of healing in writing. Imagery pulses and emanates from Don´s poetry; he handles language tools fruitfully, innovatively. An essential component of the poet´s poetry is the link of rhythm and musicality. Both elements are unavoidable for him, as he told me.

In all his greatness as a poet and person, Gutteridge is a modest human being. Alongside many other Canadian contemporary writers, Gutteridge has left a mark on what I termed in my book *Five Canadian Poets: Analytical Essays on James Deahl, John B. Lee, Don Gutteridge, Glen Sorestad, A. F. Moritz* as ***the Canadian style***.

Gutteridge´s last poem is still to be written. Let´s all wish for that. In his piece "7" (From *Where Rivers Run Deep*) he says, "… and I toss these poems / fresh-cut / on my mother's grave." Let´s hope he tosses more poems, fresh-cut, on our lives. He belongs with those iconic writers who dignify the Canadian literary mosaic, who are a part of, as John B. Lee puts forth, the "Great literature" [that] "broadens our knowledge, deepens our understanding, clarifies our emotions, and connects us to the inner wells of the self where deep need is served. In great literature we also find a meaningful connection with our fellow humans."

Don Gutteridge´s writings expand our cognition and understanding of the world, shake and set our own emotions free, and activate our nexuses with ourselves and our innermost urges. Moreover, his poetry comes from *his* connection with human beings and helps us revisit our own, substantially, indelibly, transcendently. As Christian Sia of Readers' Favorite observed (noted elsewhere before), "These poems are filled with the humanity of the writer and readers can easily relate to the emotions evoked in the lines…" *(Hidden Brook Press release)*

To conclude, I quote a longer critique by John B. Lee, in reference to *Tidings*, which condenses Gutteridge´s immeasurable quality as a writer: "I read poem after poem and think it is a masterpiece. There is an abiding sadness, but the sadness of wisdom, of knowing that if we live long enough, we lose loved ones, we keep them in our hearts though they are gone. Long ago I coined the phrase "the presence of absence" to capture in as few words as possible what I felt when I thought of those loved ones I'd lost. We preserve them in poems. We keep them alive in memory and dream. We weep and grieve and lament and celebrate. This book is profound and wise and consoling. I will be reading it again and again because it goes deep. It has the courage of autobiography without the honey trap of the confessional." *(Hidden Brook Press release)*

In a nutshell, Don Gutteridge´s poetry is *invincible ink*. Let´s toast to the man, the husband, the father, the friend, the writer, the symbol, *the* bard.

Rhymes

In my advancing age
let me still be the one
wrestling with words to wield
the world anew, to send
them dancing on some
distant dais, sylvan
with simile: the page
where all my rhymes ring
true.

Don Gutteridge

Motif in my Soul

…
the poems that visit my desk and flow through
my
pen. I am simply a vessel, and I am thankful
when the muses visit.
John B. Lee

… the perpetual prism of a poem.
Don Gutteridge

Oftentimes I have considered
what prods a motif in my soul,
that sudden tremor felt in the moment
my eyes devour a poem, sparkled as they chance
upon a perfect line, a candid remark
a suggestive twist, a splendid metaphor.
Oftentimes I have wondered
what undercurrents or muses
unleash the urge, the rush, the spur
that make my hand become a vessel
and a poem, its course.

Miguel Ángel Olivé Iglesias

Don Gutteridge's Literary Novels

by Kevin Spence

Don Gutteridge's writing style can best be described as accessible romanticism. He makes use of vivid imagery, poetic phrasing and incisive metaphor to lend emotional impact without the use of overly complex language or metaphor. Gutteridge's portfolio extends through a broad variety of settings and genres, including tragedy, comedy, historical, fantastical, or modern, offering something for most prospective readers. I would contend, however, that Don Gutteridge's novels are best read by those with an active interest in Canadian history and culture. Though a book like *The Perilous Journey of Gavin the Great* offers a witty take on a classic fable structure, the lion's share of Gutteridge's novels breathe life into the days of his boyhood in Point Edward. Gutteridge uses his life experience to explore a people, place and time through his own eyes. It is this unparalleled authenticity that makes Gutteridge's portrayals of his characters into something between fact and fiction, an immortalized recreation of the kind of people who once were. The Novels of Lambton County are an exercise in not just writing, but storytelling. Gutteridge shares pieces of himself and his origins through his prose.

Themes and Narrative

Whether ordinary or fantastical, Gutteridge uses three consistent themes and narrative tools in his books: coming of age, the importance of place, and the juxtaposition of innocence and harsh reality. Each work offers a unique perspective on what living and growing in Point Edward was like. Gutteridge's protagonists span both sexes, all ages and occupy over a century of history. There is also a look at the history of more marginalized groups around Point Edward in his largest novel, *Lily's Story.* Through the myriad perspectives involved, the Novels of Lambton County do not shy away from the darker side of its history. The inclusion of the less savoury elements of Canadian village life is connected to Gutteridge's use of juxtaposition. Even in the more comically intended novels of Gutteridge's earlier years, *Bus-Ride* and *All in Good Time,* there are ominous undertones. Through the eyes of boys and provincial village men, Gutteridge highlights not just the passing intolerance and suspicion, but the bleak insecurity of the future that frames their provincial hopes and dreams. A concise and self-contained example of this juxtaposition can be seen in Gutteridge's second novel, *All in Good Time.* In even the innocent context of a piano lesson, the reader cannot escape a reminder of their loss: "'Well, I did bring some Chopin.' He flushed, and again she was reminded of the innocence of his glance. What was she doing? Some field in France, this very moment, might be reclaiming the ripped flesh of her husband." (Gutteridge, 1980, 44) It is in this fashion that Gutteridge's dark sense of humour and tragedy remains ever-present in his novels.

Arguably the most primary theme within Don Gutteridge's novels is the importance of place. There is a single exception in the review section below, but seven of the eight novels covered in this essay are devoted to developing the history and importance of Lambton County. The villagers of The Point are inextricably linked to the land that surrounds them, both conjoining to create the "Village" as Gutteridge wants the reader to see it. The importance of place in his writing is more than a monument or frieze of his childhood, however. Gutteridge explicitly creates the Village as a microcosm of Canada.

A small piece of the gestalt that is the Canada he treasures, The Point serves as memory and metaphor, a tool to share the author's romanticized vision of his beloved childhood home and one used to explore a more universal conception of what connects Canadians. Gutteridge's tone as is that of a storyteller weaving a tale alongside the reader. His tone is one in a long Canadian tradition, both personal and largely informal, displayed prominently in his unorthodox use of pronouns. Stories about The Point, and about Canada are not from the perspective of a passive observer. Rather they are from within, providing the subjectivity that gives each novel its authentic character.

Overview and Analysis

An overview of the novelistic works of Don Gutteridge is best done in three sections: Pre-Point Edward Novels, the Novels of The Point, and the others. Both the Pre-Point Novels and the Novels of The Point feature their geographical location as a matter of chief importance. The themes and narrative through-line are as much about the development of the village itself as any of the individual characters. The Novels of The Point consist of four books: *Bus-Ride, All in Good Time, Summer's Idyll,* and *Winter's Descent.*. These books are the most sequential of Gutteridge's works, happening within roughly a decade from 1939 to the late 1940s and feature a recurring and interrelated set of characters. The Pre-Point Novels consist of two books, *How the World Began* and *Lily's Story*, a revised combination of two older works: *St. Vitus' Dance* and *Shaman's Ground.* These two books take place through from the mid-19th century to the early 20th century. The greater part of these novels takes place before Point Edward exists. Thematically, the Pre-Point novels are distinguished by a generally bleak or tragic tone. They also concern themselves with the formation of Point Edward, Canada's railway and nationhood, and the Anishinaabe/Pottawatomie people in Gutteridge's novels. The novels of The Point are characterized by the setting of the already established village of Point Edward and a tighter time-period. The last two novels covered in this essay, *Bewilderment* and *The Perilous Adventures of Gavin the Great,* do not fit easily in themes or motifs of the other five novels, and ergo are better suited to individual analysis.

How the World Began is a novel following a gentle young farm-boy by the name of Ti-Luc. It begins in the year 1794 on a small farm in the largely unsettled Lambton county. The book follows Ti-Luc's idyllic childhood in the untamed bush of Canada, his transition to adulthood, and his exposure to the unkind realities of the world outside his isolated farm. His journey is inundated with themes of trauma, loss, and purpose. Of all Gutteridge's novels, *How the World Began* might have the bleakest overall tone. It opens with violence: a vengeful Pottawatomie attack on a farmstead as they retreat from the Battle of Fallen Timbers. In one uncharacteristically violent stroke, Gutteridge introduces the reader to a very different Point Edward. He displays the historical unrest in the region, introduces Trill, Ti-Luc's adopted sister, and the parable of Carcajou and Wisakedjak, a recurring duology of First Nations god figures. Within the greater scope of the Lambton County novels, *How the World Began* serves as the prologue. It demonstrates the harshness of life before The Village through Ti-Luc's experience of war, privation, and disease. It is this series of traumas that Gutteridge uses to characterize the early Ontario community. Be it the shattering of tribal nations, the suffering of slaves, or the helplessness of a family succumbing to disease, the Pre-Point is Gutteridge's examination of cultural baggage, personal and societal. These larger traumas are paralleled by the personal ones experienced by Ti-Luc, interweaving individual and nation through tragedy. Narratively, it is through his small-scale experiences of Canada's national issues that Ti-Luc grows into adulthood and fatherhood. Chief among those coming at the hands of his brother Cal, who dreams of more than the small world beyond The Bend and enlists, finding engagement in the war of 1812. Gentle Ti-Luc, who wished for nothing beyond the borders of his farm-stead, goes out in search of his brother. Through his suffering on his journey, Ti-Luc is tempered into manhood, just as his brother is forced to face the reality of the war he had so lionized. The loss and hardship on the journey reaffirm the value of what he left behind. Ti-Luc's struggle is in the desperate wish to return to the normalcy of the past — having to cope with the tragic reality that it can never be the same, and forging on regardless.

Second in the Pre-Point books is *Lily's Story*, which follows the titular Lily Fairchild from 1845 into the early 1920s. There are two strong thematic narratives at play in *Lily's Story*. The personal story of Lily, which is concerned with loss and the will to overcome grief; and the story of Point Edward, for it is within the pages of *Lily's Story* that Gutteridge details the historical formation of the town. Through the eyes of Lily, the reader can see Point Edward grow from a river-junction shanty town into the modern village that features in later novels. *Lily's Story* can best be described as a sequence of tragic relationships. There are the personal losses of Lily herself, perpetually coming to love someone and finding them torn away by disease, war and old age. There are also the losses that serve as historical commentary on the dark past of Canada and the cost of progress. Lily, growing initially far from the more settled lands near Sarnia and London, offers insight into the lives of runaway slaves, the fading language and culture of the last free tribes, the present day Anishinaabe, and the plight of women without political agency. Just as Lily loses her loved ones, the novel details the losses of the marginalized and the down-trodden, a distinctive feature of the Pre-Point novels. In later writings, the village of Point Edward is relatively peaceful and its tragedies are few. *Lily's Story* is in some sense a monument to the loss of the people who came before. A dedication to the slaves and soldiers and Anishinaabe on whose graves the village was built. Lily's story parallels that motif. Lily, elderly and alone, experiences the final loss of her home, replaced by a literal monument for the losses of the Great War (Gutteridge 2014, 410-411)

Lily's Story is a tragedy, but one that urges an unshakeable optimism. Though she experiences incessant loss and grief, Lily always manages to find the strength and courage to move on. Her story is one of self-admitted suffering, but she explicitly endorses an optimistic philosophy. An indomitable will to keep loving despite the pain of grief:

> "Cora, you've told me more about your life and travails than any one man ought to know, and I'll be damned if I can see where you had much choice. Like most women you've been devastated by wars you never started, diseases you can't cure, and children who die on you or run off to lead their own lives without a pennyworth of gratitude. The world cares only for the species, and women bear the brunt of that reality." Cora mulled that over for a while. "May be" she said. "But I chose somethin'. Every time." "And what would that be?" "I chose to love". (Gutteridge, 2014, 502)

Lily embraces the inevitability of loss and the pain that comes with it. In a sense, each of Lily's losses, and her life itself can be interpreted as a series of 'coming of age' tales. Lily has her life torn away by tragic circumstances, and rebuilds it. Lily always chooses to craft a new life, find new things and new people to value. It is a continuum from child to elder, constantly discovering new ways to be, even if it hurts her. Lily's journey is a cyclical one. An inverse of the second narrative through-line of The Point itself. The Village moves ever forward, and the memory of what it used to be fades, save for on the pages of Gutteridge's novels.

The Novels of The Point comprise most of Gutteridge's novelistic works and share many common characteristics. Each book follows a single point of view in the late 1930s or 1940s, features a coming-of-age narrative, and explores how a village reflects the nation. Gutteridge uses perspectives of all different ages and ambitions to depict his vision of The Village, one where the reeve is also a garbage man, there is a single pub, and veterans of the war can live in quiet reprieve. The cast that Gutteridge portrays are emblematic of his broader view, where no matter how fractious or petty they can seem, the villagers adhere to a common sentiment and feeling. In portraying this unified spirit, Gutteridge also makes an explicit connection to the nation. The spirit of the village is reflective of the people, to be identified together.
In *Bus-Ride*, Gutteridge draws on The Point's love of hockey to portray the spirit of the village as representative of the nation:

> "'Hello Canada, and hockey fans in the United States!' They, like a million others on this night in March of 1939, would be content to listen, to focus all senses on a single voice, riding outward to the far

> stretches of the land, carrying in its rhythms and intonations the legends of its generation." (Gutteridge, 2019, 67)

The radio play-by- play serves as a literal and metaphorical device connecting Canadians, framing Point Edward as a single piece in a mosaic. It is through the singular will of the village that Gutteridge turns the individual characters, and by extension each individual Canadian, into the fabric of the whole.

The wreath-laying ceremony in *All in Good Time* is another symbolic and metaphorical connection. A demonstration of a common will for the patchwork villagers: "Many wept, quietly. Others stood, feeling nothing but the awesomeness of the moment as if time itself had stopped to enclose them all in the stunning fusion of a second borrowed from eternity." (Gutteridge, 1980, 159) This theme of commonality, owing to its metaphorical nature, is expressed in a similar manner across the Novels of The Point.

Coming of age, though it is featured in each individual Novel of The Point, is expressed differently each time. There are four separate coming-of-age narratives at play: boyhood identity, sexual awakening, manhood, and middle-aged reinvigoration. The first and youngest stages of this 'coming of age' spectrum are in *Summer's Idyll* and *Winter's Descent.* Gutteridge's only direct prequel/sequel, both follow the protagonist, young Will, through two important transitions in his life. *Summer's Idyll* chronicles Will as he transitions from early childhood into his adolescent years through a journey of self-discovery. The nominal story is about Will and his friends putting on a circus-esque show for their school, while the meta-narrative has the boy experiencing and losing some of his youthful wonder. *Summer's Idyll* has Will come of age through abandoning comforting childhood illusions and fantasies. Gutteridge does so by playing with appearance and reality through several sub-plots: the mysterious 'stranger,' more mundane than Will's childish imagination conjures up, the failure of his parents' marriage, and the subtly-communicated costs of war.

A direct sequel to *Summer's Idyll, Winter's Descent* has Will flourishing into youthful manhood. Where *Summer's Idyll* has Will growing past childhood whimsy to see the world for how it really is, *Winter's Descent* is his venture into that world. *Winter's Descent* is a coming of age centered around desire. Will breaks free from his shell with a newfound discovery of love, the opposite sex, and his passion for writing and reading. In embodying his desires, Will undergoes a metamorphosis, defining himself from his peers, who had constituted such an important element of his identity in *Summer's Idyll.*

Bus-Ride is the story of young Will and his transition into independent manhood. It is defined not by soft romantic discovery or self-identity, but by struggle. Bill Underhill is in constant turmoil, stuck between the mountainous expectations of the entire Village and his own unclear future. The villagers view him as their star hockey hopeful, but Bill isn't even certain he wants to play hockey (*Bus-Ride*, 2019, 18). Part of Bill's indecision comes from his powerful resentment for the constrictive, quiet life that Point Edward provides. Bill envies his father, who not only saw the world, but had "Been in the world" (*Bus-Ride*, 2019, 94) and a part of its history. Bill's journey forces him to consider his future and his freedom. In trying to find his way out of the Point, Bill considers what the village means to him as he passes into manhood and confronts an impossible decision at the outbreak of the Second World War.

All in Good Time, following Horace Macintosh, The Point's Reeve (and garbage truck driver), toys with the meaning of a coming-of-age story. Not a boy passing into manhood, the Reeve's coming of age is rather a reinvigoration. As a result of the ups and downs of his going for an ill-considered political gamble, the Reeve discovers new passions and a new purpose, decades past his boyhood. Horace, so unlike Will or Bill, is ambitious and pretentious, but learns to discard old prejudices, make himself anew, and learn to love the old again.

Bewilderment: A Novel of the Great Depression takes place in Point Edward in 1936, but shares few themes with the other Novels of The Point. As a book, *Bewilderment* is a fictionalized history. It is a means of immortalizing the everyday suffering and loss that working class people went through in a period of duress. The story follows the well-intentioned coal worker Gabe Goodfellow as he helps put on a carnival and collect bond money during the height of the Great Depression, all the while trying to care for his own family. *Bewilderment's* aim and achievement is to capture the emotional aspect of history. To see hardship and privation through Gabe's eyes and to humanize what is a matter of historical canon. The tone and themes of *Bewilderment* serve as an absurdist juxtaposition, each page filled with detail on the fallout of economic disaster, clashing against the hope and marvelous excess of a Carnival. Gutteridge reaffirms the struggle that working class families experienced in the depression, and simultaneously the reason for it. In the midst of his hardships and moral compromises, Gabe still finds love and helps bring the village together in wonder at the spectacle of the carnival. More than any of Gutteridge's other works, *Bewilderment* is beholden to its title, providing a window into the inner lives of those living in Point Edward during the Great Depression.

The Perilous Journey of Gavin the Great is Gutteridge's greatest departure from his previous works, being a foray into the genre of fantasy. In the tradition of classic fables, *The Perilous Journey of Gavin the Great* is both whimsical and dark. Set in the forest called Earthwood, it is a world populated by talking and anthropomorphized forest creatures. It follows the story of Gavin, a raccoon, and his two siblings as they flee from a great disaster that threatens to destroy the entirety of their forest home. Thematically, *The Perilous Journey* flirts with biblical allegory, featuring apocalyptic floods, a life-saving and animal-laden raft, and archetypal figures like the wily fox. It is unlike any of Gutteridge's other works in that it has no readily apparent thematic metaphors. Rather, the themes of *The Perilous Journey* are reflective of classical fables and the hero's journey. Gavin and his companions face danger and fear in a grand adventure and must triumph through their cleverness, courage and virtue. Perhaps most remarkable about *The Perilous Journey* is the tone. It combines light-hearted parody and grim danger effortlessly. One moment Gutteridge might humorously draw a comparison to the Arthurian canon when Gavin acquires a "sword" he refers to as Hex-Calibre — in reality a man's discarded hunting knife (*Gavin the Great*, 2012, 252), and in the next he might be describing the simultaneously comical and chilling beasts known as "Squeezels." Gavin's journey exists somewhere in the space of satire and genuine love for fairy-tale stories, with Gutteridge working self-aware mockery into a sincerely told story.

Conclusion

Don Gutteridge's writing, entirely separated from its cultural context, is valuable as a wholly authentic experience. He lived in the land so meticulously and lovingly crafted it into his novels. One can to this day wander the very haunts Gutteridge has written about, and walk in the footsteps of Will, Bill, or Lily. There is a timelessness to the works of Don Gutteridge even as they capture a piece of history.

Bibliography

Gutteridge, D. (1980). *All in Good Time*. Black Moss Press, Windsor.
Gutteridge, D. (1991). *How the World Began*. Moonstone Press, Goderich.
Gutteridge, D. (1993). *Summer's Idyll.* Oberon Press, Ottawa.
Gutteridge, D. (1996). *Winter's Descent.* Oberon Press, Ottawa.
Gutteridge, D. (2000). *Bewilderment.* Borealis Press Ottawa..
Gutteridge, D. (2010). *The Perilous Adventures of Gavin the Great.* Borealis Press, Ottawa.
Gutteridge, D. (2014). *Lily's Story*. Bev Editions. Toronto.
Gutteridge, D. (2019). *Bus Ride*. Bev Editions. Toronto.
Powell, R. (1974, June). Bus-Ride, Don Gutteridge: *Quill & Quire*.

Donald George Gutteridge: A Short Autobiographical Story

I was born in Sarnia General Hospital on September 30, 1937, and named (but never Christened) Donald George Gutteridge (my second name after my Uncle George McWatters). My Dad, who did not graduate grade 8 spelled it Gorge, later corrected by my mother (Margaret Grace McWatters), who graduated high school in Special Commercial. Days later moved to Point Edward, soon to take up residence upstairs in my Grandparents' house at the corner of 208 Alexander (Alexandra) Avenue and Monck (Monk) Street.

In June of 1939 my maternal grandfather, John Leonard McWatters, who began living with us, was murdered in Sarnia. No one was ever charged.

In September of 1939 my Dad joined the air force (along with my Uncle Tom Gutteridge), and was soon stationed in Ottawa, where I moved with both parents. My brother Bob (Robert William), who was born that March, stayed home in the care of his grandparents. When my Dad was sent to a Labrador posting (later Iceland), my mother and I returned home in the Spring of 1940.

During the war years I led an idyllic life as a spoiled first child. I started school at the Edward Street School (now demolished) in September 1943. In October 1944 I contracted rheumatic fever and was hospitalized for a week. The high fever opened the valves of my heart. My mother put me in the care of her gynecologist, Dr. Christie, who ordered complete bed rest for seven months. I was a precocious reader and spent my bedridden hours reading whatever I could find. I never left the bed once until May of 1945. My Dad was given leave to visit me shortly after I came home from the hospital. My mother was my faithful nurse. I returned to school to finish grade two with the support of my wonderful teacher, Mrs. Young, who brought me homework to keep me up to date. I wrote my first story for Miss McDonald, my grade three teacher, (and a poem about it in *God's Geography*). From that time on I found a group of fast friends in the village whom I have put into poems and novels. It was a great life (as the books show). I spent a lot of time in my grandfather's workshop, and adored him. In July of 1945 my Dad came home after almost six years away. We had a difficult time bonding: he was a superb athlete, I wasn't. My Dad got a job as a switchtender on the local CNR and we prospered enough for my Dad and Mom to build their own house on the Fourth Line of Sarnia. The move into the lonely countryside, away from my home village, was devastating for me. For two years my brother and I, every second week, walked to the train station and caught the bus to Point Edward, where we stayed with Gran and Gramps, and tried to keep up the fraying friendships that had been so much a part of my life.

Bob and I walked a mile and a quarter to S.S. #12, a one room country school, which I attended from Grade 6 to 8. Like most kids, I soon adjusted and found new fast friends, Bobby Cooper and Tommy Fahselt, both of whom I have written poems about. I became entranced by a grade 7 girl, Grace Leckie, who occasionally rode to school on a chestnut stallion. Miss Nelson encouraged me to keep on reading and suggested I write a Christmas play for the school. It was performed, with me as leading man (Santa, I think) in the township hall before an applauding audience. My novel, Winter's Descent is a thinly disguised account of one of my years there. I also wrote my first poem that year, about Wolfe and Montcalm (in rhyming couplets).

I entered Grade 9 at Sarnia Collegiate Institute and Technical School in the Fall of 1950. There I was bullied and unhappy, failing a subject (math) for the first time in my life. In June of 1951 my Dad was transferred to Chatham (in an effort to save his marriage) and I spent the rest of that month with my grandparents and finished Grade 9. (My chief accomplishment that year was to write my first completed novel, Pass That Puck, typed out on an Underwood borrowed from my Aunty Betty). Once again I was devastated at having to leave the friends I had made and a life I had begun to enjoy. (I have written many poems about life on the Fourth Line and friends like Bonnie and Sharon Lauer, Marilyn Matheson and others.)

I spent a lonely summer in our new Chatham house at 28 Kerr Avenue in the subdivision of Orchard Heights. In the Fall I entered Chatham Collegiate Institute where, in the smaller academic school, I soon found friends with common interests, learned to play chess and handball and did well academically (third in the class). My high school years were the usual fraught story of girl-trouble and false steps, but overall happy enough years. I had two very close friends in the school and one bosom buddy who went to the Tech school, Alvin Gehl, who loved to test out the games I invented (an obsession that lasted well into my life). Alvin has been duly celebrated in several poems, and we remain friends in our old age. During these years I wrote part of a verse play on ancient Greece, an unfinished mystery story and a similarly unfinished novel about Dutch immigrants (who peopled CCI). I wrote only one poem, a lament about the failed Hungarian Revolution. I saw myself then as becoming a novelist. For the last three summers I spent in Chatham I worked in the yard office of the local CNR and saved my money for college. On the darker side, my beloved grandfather died after a prostate operation. I was devastated. It was the first of many such deaths I would suffer over the course of a long life.

In the Fall of 1956 I entered The University of Western Ontario (UWO), registered in Honours English. I did not do well in English (an indifferent lecturer) (a B) but enjoyed college life, surprising myself by having several dates and living with five other fellows upstairs in a home on the corner of Western and Sarnia Road (a plaza now), two of whom became good friends. I joined the Hesperian Club (for English lovers), heard Northop

Frye speak to us and fell in love with my minor, History. I did little writing (except for a controversial essay I wrote for Folio, the school literary journal, "Let's Destroy the Church."

The next year was wonderful. I had Professor Ross Woodman for Romantics and fell in love with Keats and Shelley. I started to write longish poems in homage to them (several were published in Folio and fortunately have faded into obscurity.) I also loved History and Geography and made the Dean's Honour List (after which, in following years, I made little effort to replicate). My partner and I came second in the university badminton championship. Don Hair and I became good friends (and still are). Alas, my parents' marriage was breaking up. My Dad moved my mother and brother to an apartment in London, promising to follow, and simply never did. My mother had to go to work to support Bob and me through the rest of our schooling. In the summer following second year, I had a chance to go north to Red Lake and work as a solutions man in the gold mine at Balmertown. I played softball for the mine's team (third base and right field) and hit over 300. My Dad would have cheered, but for us it was too late. My Dad quit the CNR (just before being offered a superintendent's job), moved to Calgary, took up both taxidermy and the drink.

I lived with my mother for my third and fourth year at Western and was both lonely and unhappy, for her and for myself. My grades suffered and I barely made it out of fourth year. But with summer approaching in 1960, the happy thought of doing the teacher training term and getting a job and having a life, I started to write again, some poems and the beginnings of a novel (about life in Balmertown). I got a job offered to me teaching English to Grades 11, 12 and 13 at Elmira District High School in Elmira, Ontario. My real life was beginning.

I instantly fell in love with teaching. I had found one of the things I had wanted to do with my life. I also fell in love with the Home Economics teacher, Margaret Anne Barnett. Anne and I went on platonic excursions to Toronto (where she had gone to school and had connections) and soon were fully in love. I proposed on a snowy night in February 1961 in Anne's new Volkswagon. We were married by a judge in Guelph and attended a small reception for us by school friends and my mother and brother. We rented the back half (servant's quarters) of a big house (the old Drew homestead) and began our married life, driving each day from Elora to Elmira District High School. Many weekends we drove to Toronto for musicals and plays at the O'Keefe Centre. It was a wonderful winter and spring. Over 85% of my Grade 13 students passed their provincial English exam.

I had to attend the second half term of my teacher education the following summer, so we moved back to London and rented an apartment on Waterloo Street (now demolished). In mid-course I came down with a serious bout of appendicitis and had my appendix removed. A week later I was back in class, catching up and determined to finish the training. I passed with honours, and we returned to Elora for another year of teaching.

1962 was an uneventful year, marked by my decision to go back to Western for a Master's degree. Since we had not had a honeymoon the summer before, we went to Europe for a nine-week excursion, visiting England, Scotland, Ireland, France, Germany, Austria and Italy. That Fall, we rented a lovely apartment on Grand Avenue, near Ridout, and I began my new degree, falling back on our savings and a fellowship that had me teaching English 20. I loved lecturing and could envision myself doing this for a living. I did well in my courses (As) but got stalled on my M.A. thesis, mostly because I had returned to my novel about life in Balmertown and didn't know which project to focus on, with the prospect of a failed M.A. or a further term in the Fall of '63 (which we couldn't afford). Moreover, Anne was expecting our first child in June of '63. It was time to forget about writing (thesis or novel) and go to work to support my family. I got one teaching English and acting as department head in Ingersoll Collegiate. We moved to a new townhouse development on Oxford Street across from Oakridge High School and I commuted each weekday. William John Barnett Gutteridge arrived a month late (July 10) but hale and hearty. I was a father. At Ingersoll, once again I loved the teaching but crossed swords with an erratic principal. I decided I couldn't stick it out (the snowy 50-minute commute and difficult superior) and applied for a job in London. I was lucky to be offered one at Beck Collegiate, one of the best schools in the City.

I stayed at Beck for two years as an ordinary English teacher (grades 9,11,12 and 13). My mother divorced my father. My brother was teaching elementary school in Point Edward. Sometime during those two years I finished my novel and sent it to Jack McClelland. He liked it but said the entire book had not one word of dialogue. I thought that if I were to become a novelist I had better learn to write dialogue. (I learned later in the decade by taking the advice of Alice Munro: that dialogue comes naturally from the creation of strong characters put in the same room.) Meanwhile I had had my first poem published in a real magazine: "This Maple in my Fallen Yard" in the Fiddlehead (1961 or 1962 and republished in *The Village Within*). Encouraged I started to write both short lyrics about Point Edward and several long poems about the Jesuits in Huronia, Champlain and LaSalle. In 1966 I moved to Westminster Secondary School as department head and Catherine Anne Gutteridge was born on June 10. I was having some success getting my poems published in the little magazines of the period (three narratives in The Fiddlehead). Again I enjoyed teaching and running a large department. Sometime in 1967 I read *Strange Empire* by John Kinsey Howard and got to work on a series of poems about Louis Riel, eventually finishing it as *Riel: A Poem for Voices*. I sent it off to Fred Cogswell at Fiddlehead and he agreed to publish 500 copies if I would subsidize the printing. Somehow, with a growing family and a new apartment in Inglewood Park, I squeezed out $200 and my first of more than 65 books was published in 1968. I was an author.

1968 was a banner year. *Riel* was published and received two good reviews and Professor John Smallbridge went on sabbatical at the new Althouse College of Education and asked me to replace him. Earlier in that Spring we moved from Inglewood Park to a townhouse on Kipps Lane. I settled in to teaching English methods to English grads and travelling about southern Ontario following my students and supervising their classroom experience. I had found a work that I really loved. I was equally fortunate in that the next year the College expanded and I was taken on full time as an assistant professor in the English Department. That same year we moved to Victoria Street. Writing-wise I began to gather together poems I wrote about Point Edward, the first of what proved to be a lifelong obsession, and Fiddlehead Poetry Books published the collection as *The Village Within: Poems Toward a Biography*. (I will not comment on all of my books in this document, except when there is a story behind the telling. (A complete bibliography is available on my Wikipedia site.) My interest in historical figures continued with *Death At Quebec and Other Poems* (Fiddlehead 1972) (I won the UWO President's medal for title poem).

In January 1972 my mother died suddenly and I wrote a poem for her*: Saying Grace: An Elegy* (Fiddlehead 1972). But earlier in the summer of 1970 I found myself free of teaching and able to take on a major writing project. I sat in the shade of my back yard and wrote, in six or seven weeks, the first draft of a comic novel, *Bus-Ride*, published in 1974 (Nairn Publishing) and well reviewed. I have no idea where the germ for this book came from, nor had I ever seen myself as a comic writer. But I had mastered dialogue (one of the book's strengths)!

Shortly after I began to search about for historical topics for future poems. I discovered and devoured Samuel Hearnes's Journal and wrote a book-length poem on him (*Coppermine* 1973), which turned out to be a finalist for that year's Governor Generals Literary Awards. Encouraged, I wrote two more book-length historical poems, *Borderlands* and *Tecumseh,* all published, like the first, by Oberon, the most successful small literary publisher in Canada at that time. I felt I had arrived as a poet (and a minor novelist). I continued to enjoy teaching at Althouse, which became a Faculty of Education at Western and was promoted to associate professor. I continued to publish papers on educational theory and practice in English throughout my twenty-five-year career (40 articles on both pedagogy and literary criticism: details are available in my Wikipedia entry..)

Family life continued apace. Anne and I took Kate and John on a number of camping trips, visited Canadian battlefields and Fort Henry. I was ready, author-wise, for a change of direction. I had written out my interests in aboriginal figures and started to look back to The *Village Within* for inspiration. Within a year I had produced *A True History of Lambton County* (Oberon, 1977) in which I used passages of "found" material from the historical record and interweaved them with the poetry. Again the reviews were good and I had found a subject I thought I could explore deeply. I was not prepared for the several years of writer's block which followed. Desperate to continue writing poetry, I conceived a project eventually published as *God's Geography* (Brick Books 1982). In it I incorporated excerpts from *The Sarnia Observer*, original and vintage photos, and excerpts from interviews with local residents taped by my Uncle Bob. For poetry, I dredged up parts of *The Village Within* and wrote a few new pieces. It turned out to be not only the mélange of a desperate poet but my best reviewed book of poetry up to that time.

In 1978 I wrote the first of my ten "academic" books and began teaching graduate courses in English pedagogy. Then I surprised myself with another comic novel, *All in*

Good Time (Black Moss Press 1982). Then followed the driest period in my writing career. I joined The League of Canadian Poets, served on the executive, did public readings across the country, but wrote no poetry. I was dry.

Sometime in 1984 or early 1985 the germ of a new novel arrived. If I could no longer be a poet perhaps I could be a novelist. I wanted to write an historical novel (that abiding interest) from a woman's point of view and *Lily's Story* was born and pursued for two years (one of them a sabbatical). I decided to publish it myself in two volumes, *St. Vitus Dance* and *Shaman's Ground* (1986 and 1988). The books are set in Lambton County and Point Edward, continuing my interest in local history. (In 2014 Bev Editions published the two volumes as *Lily's Story)* Novel writing continued with another historical novel, *How the World Began: A Parable of 1812* (Moonstone 1991.) The highlight of 1985 was the birth of my first grandson, followed a few years later by the birth of three more grandsons and even later by two granddaughters and since then they have been the highlight of my life. Tom lived with us for six years until Kate married, and when he was old enough we travelled with him widely, and he has inspired a number of poems over the years

In 1991 Oberon published a slim volume of verse, *Love in the Wintertime.* But again I turned to fiction as my main focus. And returned to my home village. Out came two memoir novels, *Summer's Idyll* and *Winter's Descent* (1993 and 1996) In between them I wrote a children's/young adult novel, *The Perilous Journey of Gavin the Great* (not published until 2011 by Borealis). I published one other book of poetry in this period. But I was also coming to the end of a long academic career. I retired in October 1993.

Bored with retirement, I started in on what became a twelve-volume mystery series, *The Marc Edwards Mysteries*, with four publishers over a twelve-year period (2003-2015). These would be the last prose I would write. But I started writing poems again. The principal focus in these numerous volumes (12 titles over 20 years and three more to come) was Point Edward with many occasional poems added, on family life, the process of writing itself and aspects of my aging. My style also evolved. I began writing short poems that gradually were subsumed by internal rhyme, assonance, consonance and alliteration, unlike the more free flowing lyrics of the earlier period with "natural" line breaks. I continue to write these somewhat old-fashioned poems. It's been a full life.

About the Author
Miguel Ángel Olivé Iglesias

Miguel is the Ambassador Editor-in-chief and president in Cuba of the Canada Cuba Literary Alliance (CCLA). He does translation, proofreading, reviewing and revision for the CCLA, along with compilation and anthologizing. He is a member of the Mexican Association of Language and Literature Professors, VP of the William Shakespeare Studies Center and member of the Canadian Studies Department of the Holguín University in Cuba. He is an Associate Professor at the University of Holguín, with a Bachelor's degree in Education, Major in English, and a Master's degree in Pedagogical Sciences. He has been teaching for thirty-two years and writing literary reviews, poems and stories in Spanish and English. Miguel has written and published numerous academic papers in Cuba, Mexico, Spain and Canada. So far he has published more than a hundred poems, four short stories and over thirty-five critical reviews of poetry books and novels in different issues. The author and editor is currently involved in many CCLA projects. He works in the Teacher Education English Department as a professor of English, English Stylistics and grad courses. He is also Head of the English Language Discipline. He uses his academic papers, essays, stories and poems in class for reading, debating and practicing the language, adding a didactic and formative element to his scientific and literary production. He also does poetry reading in co-curricular on-campus and community activities

Latest publications:
Author and Translator. (Poetry) *Forge of Words / Fragua de palabras.* Hidden Brook Press. 2020.
Author. (Literary Critique) *In a Fragile Moment: A Landscape of Canadian Poetry.* Hidden Brook Press. 2020.
Author and Essayist. (Literary Critique) "Instants of a People's Poet Titan: A Review of Some of Milton Acorn's Poems in *In a Springtime Instant*" in *Canadian Stories* magazine (Volume 23, No. 131) pp. 70-72, February/March, 2020.
Author, Reviewer, Translator and Editor. (Poetry) *The Divinity of Blue.* CCLA Visit to Cuba 2020. Hidden Brook Press. 2020.
Translator, Reviewer and Editor. (Poetry) *Flying on the Wings of Poetry / Volando en las alas de la poesía.* Hidden Brook Press. 2020. (John B. Lee, Antony Di Nardo, Laurence Hutchman, Richard Marvin Grove)
Editor, Translator and Essayist. (Poetry) Bridges Series Books, Book V *The Heart Upon*

the Sleeve / Emociones al descubierto. Hidden Brook Press. 2021. (Lourdes González, John B. Lee, Roberto Manzano, Richard Marvin Grove)
Editor, Translator, Author. (Scientific Papers) *Pedagogical Sciences. The Teaching of Language and Literature, Education, Values, Patrimony and Applied IT.* QuodSermo Publishing. 2021.
Author, Editor and Essayist. (Literary Critique) *Five Canadian Poets: Analytical Essays on James Deahl, John B. Lee, Don Gutteridge, Glen Sorestad, A. F. Moritz.* QuodSermo Publishing. 2021.
Editor, Author. (Literary Critique) *On the Breeze of Canadian Literature: International Reviews and Essays.* QuodSermo Publishing.
Author, Editor, Essayist. (Literary Critique) *A Shower of Warm Light. Reviews and Essays on Canadian Poetry.* Hidden Brook Press.

Work in progress:
Author, Editor and Translator. (Poetry) *This Pulse of Life, These Words I Found.* SandCrab Books.

References

ALEXANDER, Becky D. Quotation *IN* "The Confederation Poets: The Founding of a Canadian Poetry, 1880 to the First World War." Paper written by Canadian poet, essayist and scholar, James Deahl.
Babylon English, Digital Dictionary.
BROWN, E. K. *On Canadian Poetry.* Toronto: McGraw-Hill Ryerson, 1943. Print. Reprinted in 1973 by The Tecumseh Press.
Digital Concise Oxford English Dictionary.
Digital Merriam-Webster Collegiate® Dictionary.
DRAGLAND, Stanley. "Al Purdy's Poetry: Openings." *IN Al Purdy. Essays on his Works.* Guernica Editions. 2002. Edited by Linda Rogers.
ECO, Umberto. *The Name of the Rose* (*Il nome della rosa*). Bompiani Harcourt. Italy. 1981.
GALPERIN, I. R. *Stylistics.* Moscow Vyssaja Skola. 1981.
Hidden Brook Press release. Press Release and Onix Information. Don Gutteridge´s book *Point Taken.*
Holy Bible. Zondervan Publishing House. 1984.
LEE, John B. Poem "Kissing the Darkness When the Pages Close."
LEE, John B. Poems "One Leaf in the Breath of the World, "I Wake to Breathe Your Beauty In." *IN This is How We See the World.* Hidden Brook Press. 2017.
MEZEI, Kathy. https://www.britannica.com/biography/Anne-Michaels. Article.
OLIVÉ IGLESIAS, Miguel Ángel. *In a Fragile Moment: A Landscape of Canadian Poetry.* Hidden Brook Press. 2020.
OLIVÉ IGLESIAS, Miguel Ángel. *Five Canadian Poets: Analytical Essays on James Deahl, John B. Lee, Don Gutteridge, Glen Sorestad, A. F. Moritz.* QuodSermo Publishing. 2021.
OLIVÉ IGLESIAS, Miguel Ángel. *A Shower of Warm Light. Essays and Reviews on Canadian Poetry.* Hidden Brook Press. (work in progress)
POE, Edgar Allan. Line from his poem "The Raven." *IN The Literature of the U.S.A.* Editorial Pueblo y Educación. Cuba. 1983.
SHAKESPEARE, William. Quotation from *Complete Works of William Shakespeare.* (Volume XVIII). Philadelphia David McKay, Publisher.
SORESTAD, Glen. Fragment from his poem "Six Reasons I Write Poems." *IN A Thief of Impeccable Taste.* SandCrab Books. 2011.
SPENCE, Kevin. *Home Ground: Don Gutteridge's Literary Novels.* Literary critique.
TWAIN, Mark. *The Adventures of Tom Sawyer.* American Publishing Company. 1876.
VOA Learning English. Adam Brock, writer and producer. Ashley Thompson, editor.

Appendix

As an enriching accompaniment to the analyses made in this book, I included the insights of Kevin Spence in his article *Home Ground: Don Gutteridge's Literary Novels on page 90.* The paper deeply explores Don Gutteridge's novels, offering the reader a comprehensive, knowledgeable view necessary to further know the man and his oeuvre.

CanLit Revealed

A Series of Review and Essay Books on Canadian Literature.

Title: *In a Fragile Moment: A Landscape of Canadian Literature*

ISBN – 978-1-927725-92-4 – Softcover
ISBN – 978-1-927725-93-1 – epub
ISBN – 978-1-927725-94-8 – mobi

Publisher: QuodSermo Publishing

In a Fragile Moment is an insightful collection of essays and reviews, written from the poetic heart of Professor Olivé. The authors covered in this astute critical study are treated with heart felt respect. Professor Olivé has the uncanny ability to portray his incisive observations in a poetic and perceptive manner.

Title: *A Shower of Warm Light: Reviews and Essays on Canadian Literature*
Author: M.Sc. Miguel Ángel Olivé Iglesias

ISBN – 978-1-989786-55-0 (softcover)
ISBN – 978-1-989786-56-7 (ebook)

Publisher: QuodSermo Publishing

A Shower of Warm Light follows in the footsteps of *In a Fragile Moment* as a profoundly insightful collection of reviews and essays by M.Sc. Miguel Ángel Olivé Iglesias on Canadian Literature. Professor Olivé continues to open the readers eyes to the warm light of contemporary Canadian Literature.

Title: *On the Breeze of Canadian Literature: International Reviews and Essays*
Editor: M.Sc. Miguel Ángel Olivé Iglesias

ISBN – 978-1-989786-45-1 (softcover)
ISBN – 978-1-989786-46-8 (ebook)

Publisher: QuodSermo Publishing

On the Breeze of Canadian Literature follows in the tradition of In a Fragile Moment and A Shower of Warm Light but this time as an international collection of reviews and essays by scholars, professors and academics from around the world. Through these well written and accessible essays Professor Olivé brings us an enlightening perspectives on Canadian Literature.

Title: *Ploughing the Home Ground: Essays on Canadian Literature and Poetics*
Author: Don Gutteridge

ISBN – 978-1-989786-59-8 (softcover)
ISBN – 978-1-989786-60-4 (ebook)

Publisher: QuodSermo Publishing

Ploughing the Home Ground is a collection of republished essays on Canadian Literature and Poetics by Don Gutteridge including two essays about Don and his work.

Title: *Five Canadian Poets: Analytical Essays on, James Deahl, John B. Lee, Don Gutteridge, Glen Sorestad, A. F. Moritz*
Author: M.Sc. Miguel Ángel Olivé Iglesias

ISBN – 9781989786369 (softcover)
ISBN – 9781989786376 (ebook)

Publisher: QuodSermo Publishing

Here you will find outstanding essays on both the biographical history as well as the literary history of five of Canada's top poets. This collection of essays brings literary life to Canadian poetry in the making. Examples of each poet's work are critiqued, examined and observed gently and sympathetically. They have been described as "well-researched love letters to poetry and the poetic spirit." These essays will open your eyes to poetry.

Title: *The Canadian Poet Who Wrote Himself Whole: Revealing the Poetics of Don Gutteridge*
Author: M.Sc. Miguel Ángel Olivé Iglesias

ISBN – 978-1-989786-57-4 (softcover)
ISBN – 978-1-989786-58-1 (ebook)

Publisher: QuodSermo Publishing

The Canadian Poet Who Wrote Himself Whole is a fine collection of essays and reviews by scholar and essayist Miguel Ángel Olivé Iglesias on the poetry and prose of world class Canadian poet Don Gutteridge.

www.ingramcontent.com/pod-product-compliance
Lightning Source LLC
Chambersburg PA
CBHW080452030726
47592CB00011B/3079

9781989786574